Redefining Normal

A Modern Gay Man's Guide to Happy and Healthy Living

BRENT HEINZE, LPC

FOREWORD BY RACE BANNON

Edited by Nic Garcia

Cover graphic design provided by
Bruce Galardi (bruce.galardi@xlur8.org)

Author image provided by
Wayne D. Lewis (happydog63creative.com)

Cover models
Jesse Jackman (www.JesseJackman.xxx)
Dirk Caber (www.DirkCaber.com)

Photograph used by permission from
FLYFOTO (www.FlyFotoImages.com)

Original versions of these writings were published in Out Front and are
included here in cooperation with Q Publishing Group, Inc.

To all the wonderful people in my life
that I am fortunate enough to call friends.

ACKNOWLEDGMENT

The creation of this anthology of my writings has been supported by some extremely important people in my life. The Out Front Colorado family has backed me in difficult times, done their best to aid me in becoming a better writer and pushed me to develop more confidence in expressing my perspectives. They have been an industry leader in gay publications and are currently celebrating their 40th year of producing the country's top two longest running gay magazines. These columns are printed with kind permission of Out Front's owners and publishers. I want to thank Jay Klein, Jerry Cunningham, JC McDonald, Matt Kailey, Nic Garcia, Holly Hatch, Matt Pizzuti, and Berlin Sylvestre for challenging and encouraging me in my efforts to have a positive impact in our community and culture through my writing. Nic also offered his passion for writing and an incredible amount of patience with me as the editor for this collection.

This book is dedicated to a few people that have showed me amazing friendship and understanding throughout my life. The love and stability from my relationship with my partner Todd has been crucial in allowing my creative dreams to become a reality. He holds down the fort, provides tech support, and comforts me when I get overwhelmed. My mom Hope's tenacity and sense of humor gave me the foundation to grow into a man that I am proud of today. The rest of my chosen and biological families have supported me by providing opportunities to discuss all of the wild ideas I have in my head and offer much needed down time when I can be convinced to take some. They provide authentic compassion, affection and laughter in my life. Alan Cook, Bruce Rumsey, and Julie Bellum empowered me to continue finding confidence in developing my therapeutic voice. I would also like to express my gratitude to Race Bannon, Dave Johnson, Scot Solida, Ben Gilliam, Brandon Campbell, David Corder, Christopher Grano, Christopher Maher, Steve D'Ascoli,

Shannon Campbell, Janet Rose, Jacob Warner, Bob Dorsheimer, Dan Brown, Michael Beatty, and Dave Watt for inspiring, supporting, and pushing me to continue writing and follow my passion to aid others in their own journey of personal development.

I also want to acknowledge a few nameless individuals who caused disruption to happen in my life through what felt like extremely catastrophic, hurtful, and destructive ways. In retrospect, they provided opportunities for me to have my world shaken up so I had to step out of my somewhat comfortable existence and have to modify my plans. They taught me to be flexible and adaptable so I could develop the confidence to deal with adversity. I became more accepting of the idea that injury, pain and discomfort are natural parts of facing challenges and trying new things. These experiences were difficult, distressing, and incredibly important for me to work through. I was able to take something positive out of these challenging moments instead of becoming resentful of them and shutting down. They were crucial to my personal development.

Lastly, an enormous amount of appreciation and admiration goes out to all who have read my columns and are working to improve their lives. It takes courage to challenge yourself in making personal changes. Some of these tasks appear larger or tougher than others, but the belief you can accomplish a goal is the strongest indicator of your own success. Don't let fear of failure or a history of difficulty stop you from creating an amazing life full of happiness and fulfillment. Continue traveling on your path to a successful future and enjoy the process you have undertaken while you make fantastic friends along the way.

CONTENTS

Contents

Contents

FOREWORD

*"Normal is an illusion. What is normal
for the spider is chaos for the fly."*
— Morticia Addams

People dole out advice all the time. Parents. Teachers. Friends. Coworkers. Bosses. Spiritual leaders. Therapists. They all give advice and ultimately there are but a few yardsticks by which we judge the quality of that advice: knowledge, experience and trustability. Brent Heinze possesses all three of those qualities in massive quantities, and that's why I so vehemently endorse the contents of this book.

Let me add one more quality that Brent embodies fully - empathy. Empathy is perhaps the most cherished and important of human abilities allowing one to truly role reverse with another person and feel what they're feeling, or at least have a genuine sense of that person's experience. Brent has the enviable ability to converse with someone or hear of their particular circumstances and tap into how they feel and how to best navigate that particular territory. That skill set is evidenced throughout Brent's writings.

As explained elsewhere here, Brent's own life history has not always been one of an easy, confident or self-accepting path. Owning up to his own challenges and how he learned from them is part of why he's such a good therapist and able to relate to his clients and readers so well. Are you experiencing a bumpy time? Has life thrown you a curve ball or two? Brent's been there also, and he's well-equipped to offer assistance to help you better surmount those challenges.

I must also come clean that Brent is a good friend of mine. We have been friends for many years. If you were to know me personally, you'd know that I choose my close friends wisely. Someone of less quality may circle within my sphere of social acquaintances, but they are never relegated to good friend status. Brent is a good friend and good people. My admiration of him is unequivocal.

As I've read the drafts of this book in preparation for its publishing, my admiration for him as a writer has taken up residence alongside my admiration for him personally. I consider myself a fairly decent writer and I don't laud someone's writing easily. So what you're about to read not only contains wise and useful words, but words crafted to land nicely upon the eyes and mind as well.

Ostensibly this book is targeted at LGBT folks, but the truth is the range of the human experience tends to cross demographics more than it does not. Ultimately we're all people. We all share in this thing called the life experience. As you read what follows, you'll see the advice offered in this book tends to apply to a broader demographic regardless of how they identify their gender or sexual orientation. It might be touted as a gay man's guide to happy and healthy living, but the commonalities we all share as human beings often transcend orientation. Just about anyone will find value in this book.

I also remain acutely aware that our LGBT culture is

unique with its own set of challenges, perspectives, expectations, history, pitfalls, tragedy, and beauty. Brent highlights those aspects of life that will resonate with LGBT folks for sure, but woven amidst those insights are gems of wisdom that any person walking the face of the Earth will find thought provoking and helpful.

Now, let's talk about normal, since the book's title ostensibly "redefines normal." Whether Brent is writing about sex, dating, community, emotional challenges, or any of the many topics encompassed within the dozens of columns in this book, what he always does is honor the uniqueness in each of us. What he does not do is pigeonhole his reader into neat little boxes of normality that serves no one very well. Brent lives up to my favorite quote of all time by Dr. Seuss, "Today you are You, that is truer than true. There is no one alive who is Youer than You." (Isn't that just an awesome quote?)

So, why is redefining normal important to do? Whenever such a question is posed, it always reminds me of a line Stockard Channing says in the movie Practical Magic. "Being normal isn't necessarily a virtue...it rather denotes a lack of courage." Brent is himself courageous, and his work constantly encourages others to be courageous too.

The value of what Brent does, challenging the destructive nature of normality, and the way people cling to it for security like a life raft, does a great service to anyone within his sphere, including those who read his work such as the book in front of you now.

Clinging to the misguided notion that being normal, being "just like everyone else," is somehow a gold standard for which to aim is one of the prime reasons people's lives sometimes succumb to a downward spiral. Such an attitude often engenders shame, sadness, depression, and feelings of "being the other." If you happen to be gay, lesbian, bisexual, transgender, queer, pansexual, polyamorous, or any of the other alternative identifications we place upon ourselves, you are by default "not normal."

But let me be quite clear, and it's the reason why much of what you'll read in this book applies to anyone regarding of gender or sexual orientation. No one is normal. No one. Not a single human being matches up to all of the normal, middle of the road and mainstream characteristics, personality traits, mindsets, sexualities, relationship styles or world views. Every one of us is truly unique, unlike anyone else. This is why thinking and writing like Brent's is so valuable.

The very notion of normality is laughable when properly dissected. Essentially, elevating the value of being normal to its logical end result means many believe in the correctness of being average. To be normal is to be average. Of course, the average individual does not exist. Each individual is unique. Average characteristics are a statistical tool that cannot be applied to any individual. So many variables are involved in an individual's character, physical structure, and psychological makeup that no individual can possibly be an average person. Moreover, no average psychology or lifestyle exists.

Anytime we try to quantify or measure an individual's makeup by any set of standards, they are destined to fall short. In spite of the pressure around to all try to be the same, we just aren't. And this is what makes life worth living. How boring if we truly all were the same. There would be nothing new to learn, explore or experience.

Even traditional psychotherapeutic strategies are increasingly accepting the concept of individual uniqueness. Transpersonal psychology, for example, attempts to embrace this more comprehensive view of human nature. We simply must accept that it's the celebration of the uniqueness in us all that's the elixir of a happy and rewarding life. Anything less will impact us negatively.

The opposite of expressing your personal uniqueness is to constantly work to "cover up" our true natures. A gay man who remains in the closet for fear of not being normal. Someone who enjoys the kinkier side of sex remains mired in shame because some mental programming they've endured has told them it's wrong. When someone finds happiness in a non-traditional relationship configuration or dynamic, they are forever challenged to defend their happiness in such a situation because it's not normal.

When we accept that such covering up and closeting is an appropriate response to the social messaging that being normal is the ideal, we suffer. Not only do we suffer, but all of society suffers as well. Each human being has their own strengths, weaknesses, talents and points of view. If we worship at the altar of normality, we deprive ourselves and those around us of an important part of nature.

So what does this all mean? Be you! Don't try to be who someone else thinks you should be. It is only by fully accepting your uniqueness, honoring it, embracing it, that you can attain maximum happiness and contentment. There is no other way. You simply can't live your life on someone else's terms and expect to be happy. It won't happen. Celebrate uniqueness.

Who else thinks this way? Who else wants you to honor and revel in your uniqueness, you not being normal? Brent Heinze, the author of this beautiful book you are about to embark on reading. I guarantee you that you'll be a changed person by the time you read the last page. A changed person for the better. And isn't that what we all want in life?

Enjoy. Let the words of Brent's wisdom wash over you like the warmth of sunshine illuminating a brighter future. You'll be glad you undertook the journey.

Race Bannon
San Francisco
March 2016

INTRODUCTION

Late in 2010, I was contacted by Matt Kailey, the editor of Out Front, about using my counseling experience, love of leather and unique sense of humor to create a relationship column that focused on addressing questions and issues affecting the gay male community. His request freaked me out. I considered myself a solid speaker, but had never written professionally or taken much of an opportunity to take my mental pile of random thoughts and impressions, organize them, and present them in a meaningful written way. Words usually just spew from my mouth, sometimes making friends and people around me giggle or raise an eyebrow. I endeavored to create something that would amuse, empower, provoke, challenge, and provide opportunities for readers to ponder future possibilities. These columns were intended to make people think about their lives, realize that they are not alone in their struggles, and enable them to take better control of their emotions, choices, and happiness. Simply put, I wanted to help give other people ideas, tools, and a kick in the butt they could use to create a fantastic life.

Writing *HeinzeSight* allowed me to express ideas my brain wrestles with throughout the day and often in my dreams while I try to get a full night of sleep. I conceptualize struggles many gay people experience, but also realize most can be applied to broader society regardless of gender or sexual orientation. I also remain aware our gay culture is unique with its own set of challenges, perspectives, expectations, history, pitfalls, tragedy, and beauty. Whether readers identify as gay, straight, or anywhere in between, I wanted to create opportunities for people to think about ways to change their lives.

We all go about our daily existence in ways that are considered "normal" for us, even if we don't feel these patterns are entirely desirable. My goal is for people to stop and think about their lives and the choices they make. So many times, we run from one situation to the next, trying to get through each day with little thought about how to make deeper and longer-lasting improvements in our lives. We tackle challenges often only to get through them and move on to the next ones. We run toward an unclear and undefined future because we haven't taken time to figure out what gets us excited to wake up each day ready to attack the world. We also haven't worked to identify many of the barriers keeping us from finding fulfillment.

The time I've spent writing these columns has been a wild ride that impacted me in ways which I could have never foreseen. There is a fair amount of notoriety that makes the ego-driven part of my personality jump up and down with excitement, but there is much more of a philanthropic benefit to my efforts. I want to help create opportunities for people to make life-changes. These improvements allow for more happiness in our own lives and can act as an encouraging force for others around us. When enough cheerful, healthy, empowered people exist within a population, the larger society can also benefit and thrive.

This understanding of our own ability to create amazing lives came through many trials of my own. Many aspects of my life are public and I openly enjoy sharing those. Like everyone else, there are also things that exist below my surface that people usually don't have an opportunity to see. Many of my columns reflect my own past or current insecurities, frustrations, realizations, and hopes for the future. Most people who know me in this current phase of my life find it hard to believe that I used to be devastatingly shy with extremely low self-esteem. My own journey in developing confidence to engage with people socially and face my own challenges with self-confidence only started when I was about 30-years-old. Before that, I struggled with accepting myself and visualizing how I would ever be truly happy.

I was the quintessential shy, awkward, gay, intelligent, introverted, timid, and self-loathing spooky goth kid and felt I was not a viable part of any groups around me. That was my personal "normal." Fitting in with the majority of other kids was laughable. I usually took opportunities to hang out with adults or chose to spend time by myself reading or listening to music in my room.

Although my Grandma Edie supported my love of literature, as a kid, I idolized my grandfather for many things, but especially his ability to grip an audience with a story or land an amazingly hilarious joke. Pop could enter an event where he did not know anyone and within an hour he was surrounded by a new group of friends. This drove me to try to be as charismatic as he was, but unfortunately I did not have much natural aptitude for this. It didn't get much better through the remainder of public school and my lack of these social skills followed me through college and into adulthood.

Eventually, I became friendly with a few people who actually enjoyed hanging out with me for my quirky personality and variety of interests. While I was beginning to feel like I could be myself around people, I was still far from unapologetically putting myself out there for all to see.

In 2004, I began a ten-year journey to pursue a completely new adventure of self-acceptance and strength-building. It all started with the end of an almost nine-year relationship. This left me feeling even more unsure and insecure about myself. My desire to connect with others socially and my general trust in people massively declined. I had a choice to live in a place of bitterness where I saw the world as being an unfair place that continued to show very little love or compassion for me, but I took a different route. I decided to take life with both hands, jump on, and prepare for an amazing ride.

I decided it was important for me to face some of my insecurities and learn how to talk to people so I could make friends. I practiced starting conversations with people I didn't know and took opportunities to talk to people who intimidated me. Over time, I began to feel more confident that connecting with people was not only possible, but also could be fun. Strangely enough, a series of leather-centered experiences propelled me quickly toward a large growth spurt in my life - running for Mr. Leather Colorado.

I had never felt the desire to compete in one of these contests. I was fairly vocal about how I felt they were an unnecessary part of our community and nothing that I wanted to pursue. One primary idea changed my perspective and drove my decision to put myself out publically in this way. I had reached a point in my life where I had begun to achieve true happiness and feelings of success. I was now able to articulate my inner motivation to set life-changing goals and how I was able to accomplish these changes. It felt important for me to express it openly. The contest provided a chance to do that.

I became Mr. Leather Colorado 2010. Soon after, I competed at International Mr. Leather in Chicago. During the third day of the contest I found out that I made it into the Top 20 and would have the opportunity to make a speech about something important to me. It went like this:

I think we've been lied to. We've been told that to "give up" shows weakness. I've actually improved my life by learning to give up and I believe that we can all benefit from this philosophy. First of all, give up that our social lives revolve around being online. Get offline, get out, meet up, and get off with someone. Give up the idea that you're not buff, furry, tattooed, or successful enough to talk to that hot guy over there. Just go over and say "hi." Self-confidence is really damn sexy. Give up the idea that you have to fit a particular image to be accepted. Take the time to figure out who you truly are and what you're really about. Give up using terms like "clean" that discriminate against us. I got educated and won't let the fear of a virus dictate who I love or screw. Like so many of us, I had to find the courage to become comfortable with myself and give up those things that kept me feeling insecure and scared. My journey of becoming a strong man has been shaped by this simple idea and I present myself living a life of gratitude, integrity, and passion. It all started by learning how to just give up.

I got a standing ovation and made my partner cry in the audience. More importantly, I got to publically announce this discovered philosophy that truly embodied so much of what I had come to understand about what was keeping me back from creating a great life for myself. My "normal" life wasn't one that I was ultimately happy with, so it was up to me to try to create something different. It was important to let go of some of the old crap that I had been hoarding inside for so many years. I also had to work on developing new skills that would benefit me in making strong relationships. This success wasn't just going to fall in my lap. It was going to take work and determination.

Looking back, it took me many years and a huge dedication of energy and effort to transform those parts of myself that kept me trapped and miserable internally, but also stopped me from trying to connect with other people. I took opportunities to understand, heal, and grow from the trials of my past to become a confident man and to appreciate myself for all my strengths, insecurities, and uniqueness. There were times I had convince myself that these struggles for self-improvement were worth it and it was important to keep working on those things even when I thought it was too difficult or pointless.

"Redefining Normal: A Modern Gay Man's Guide to Happy & Healthy Living" is an anthology of my first 100 *HeinzeSight* columns written for Out Front Colorado magazine during 2011-2015. Although these columns were previously printed, I have expanded each narrative since the initial versions were limited by word counts and space limitations. This provided a much-appreciated opportunity for me to review each topic to see how my perspectives have changed throughout the years and enhance ideas previously presented. This process of writing and editing created a reflective place where emotions of pride, excitement, disbelief, and humbleness bubble inside me. I am truly honored to have the opportunity to publish this book and share these ideas with a broader audience.

Through my interactions, I've seen many individuals take control of their lives, develop new skills to deal more effectively with the world around them, and forge stronger relationships. I'm honored to lend my experience as a counselor paired with a sarcastic and sometimes twisted sense of humor and conglomeration of life experiences to write about issues faced by many of us.

This collection represents my desire to support people in our community, but is also reflective of how far I have come in facing my own set of challenges. I am confident we all have the ability to evolve in ways that support our creation of a life we love living. We can form stronger relationships, gain higher degrees of success and enjoy our time more while we are alive. Sometimes we just need to start the process by taking opportunities to take a hard look at ourselves and decide it is the right time to begin working on those aspects of our lives keeping us down. There is no time like right now, so get moving. Start redefining your normal.

CHAPTER 1: DATING

Looking for love

Dear Brent,

I have been looking for someone to date for a long time and I feel like just giving up. I put myself out there socially, both in person and online with little success. I've had some OK dates, but none of them have resulted in anything significant. It seems that the good guys are already taken or only looking for a disconnected one-night stand. Of course, the tragic ones want to get into a relationship very soon after meeting me. It doesn't seem like I can find the guys that I enjoy hanging out with. I know my attitude toward dating is dropping into a really negative space quickly and I fear that my desire to find a partner may be fading as well. What am I doing wrong and how can I find more of the right guys?

I have often heard the adage that "you find love when you're not looking for it." I don't think the universe works that way, but there are probably some reasons why love appears to happen often when we least expect it. There are times when we are vigorously looking to achieve something that we really want. This process can't happen fast enough for us and we may risk becoming impatient with the time it is taking. In these situations, getting to the destination is much more important to us then experiencing the journey. During times where you are on the prowl for a husband, you may lose sight of the importance in experiencing the process of finding compatible people, both romantically and for friendship.

Be aware of how you may come across to others when you are on this expedition. Your body language and words could communicate your hopes for success and frustrations with past encounters, but also an urgency that you are putting out while you are looking for someone. When you enter a place, you may look pretty intense when you are scanning the room. There may be less of a chance you are smiling since you are on the hunt. You might also miss that you're being checked out or just got shot a quick smile from some cute guy. You may also show impatience, discouragement, and grumpiness when talking to people if you're in a desperate or negative headspace. It's amazing how these seemingly minor things sneak out of us, even if you don't intentionally intend them.

When you do connect with someone, there could also be tendencies to feel that you have to scrutinize the interaction to determine if they are meeting enough of your minimum requirements to consider this date a success or have scored enough points to win a second date with you. If you are focused on maintaining a tally sheet, you are not being fully present in the moment and are most likely experiencing the enjoyment of the date. Be careful not to give up too early. There have been times for all of us where we have been on a date and thought that the guy was nice, but there was no romantic spark. Sometimes our over-analysis can keep us from giving someone a chance and you may be missing an opportunity to get to know an amazing person, even if it is only to have a little fun. Unless you're psychic, quit convincing yourself that you can see into the relationship magic ball and see the future that this person absolutely will not be a positive part of your life, either for a relationship, friendship, or to act as some other supportive person.

When you are so focused on finding a relationship, you risk losing the enjoyment of the dating process and getting to know people. If your heart or mind is shut down after the first inkling that the person is not worth pursuing, the remainder of the date is pointless and a total downer. Work on enjoying someone for what they bring to the table at that moment. You may be discounting someone too early by not giving them a chance. Even if they are not "the one," they may prove to be a cool person or turn you on to someone that may be a more compatible one for you.

There are also times when we find love in someone that doesn't fit our preconceived idea of what he will look like or when he will magically appear in our lives. It is so important to keep your eyes, mind, and heart open to the possibility that there are wonderful people out there that will enrich our lives, but maybe not in the way we initially thought they would. Even if this change in perspective does not land you a partner immediately, it can increase your enjoyment of connecting with people and could gain you some great new friends and experiences.

Another thing to remember is that social networking can be a powerful tool in your dating arsenal. Even if your date doesn't turn out to be Prince Studmuffin, he may invite you to a party where you meet someone else that turns you on to a great new restaurant where you go and enjoy the veal which starts a conversation with the guy next to you that is eating the same thing who coincidentally just had his friend cancel on him for the Erasure concert that night and he asks you if you want to go with him.

Give until it hurts

Dear Brent,

I think I'm better looking than average and a great catch. Often I develop a relationship with someone and have a tendency to give them everything I think they need and want. Unfortunately when it comes to reciprocation, I'm left completely unfulfilled after I've become emotionally bonded to them. They don't do wonderful things for me after I have been so thoughtful. I feel frustrated because people around me don't seem to care about what I want. How can I find someone who cares about my happiness?

I can understand the enjoyment of seeing the looks on people's faces when they feel excited about something you did for them. We may not communicate what we honestly want from situations to other people, especially within a relationship. Those in our lives may be left to their own perceptions of what they think we want or deserve. They could guess wrong or do something that effectively hurts us and impacts our feelings of fulfillment in the relationship. Other times, we pick the wrong person to perform a particular set of expectations that make us feel validated. It may not be normal for them to be sweet and thoughtful, but we may continue to pray that they will miraculously transform into that perfect version of what we want them to become.

One of the perils of being tuned in to what will make other people feel good is that there are times where we may lose sight of what makes us feel contented. Maybe we have never taken the opportunity to really discover what turns our crank or makes us happy in our lives. Some people grow up with the idea that pleasing other people earns them acceptance, friendship, and favoritism. Pleasing other people is a nice thought when it is not done as a method to simply get what we want or through sacrificing our own desires. This can cause a loss of focus about what truly makes us feel happy and may lead into developing bitterness and anger when people seemingly don't care since efforts aren't reciprocated. Although this is often not the case, it may feel that way to those who never seem to get their way. There is a huge difference between doing something nice for someone and giving excessively over and over.

Another concern is giving someone everything they want and expecting a particular benefit in return. It is a similar pitfall when using a bastardized version of the Laws of Attraction as a mantra. This law can be simplified down to good things happen to those who do good things for others by attracting positive people and situations into our lives. One of the problems that can arise if you have a misguided viewpoint of this philosophy is to expect good things to happen to you just because you deserve them since you did something that you feel was worthy of a payback. You risk getting bitter and demotivated when this cosmic reciprocation doesn't happen fast enough or in the way that you hope it will come back. Being a thoughtful and kind person should be its own reward, but we all hope to get something good out of situations. Purchasing Diesel jeans for a friend on their birthday will hopefully not be reciprocated with a pair of close-out sale sweatpants from Wal-Mart, but it could happen. Be careful of disappointment.

Take some time to sit back and think about what you are really trying to accomplish when doing all these thoughtful things for others. Consider if you are doing these because of an internal desire to give to someone else or if you expect something specific from them in return. Although these guys may be missing out on a good thing with you, make sure that you aren't trying to bolster your own confidence and self-worth through attempts to gain their dedication through these actions. Take the time to get to know them before giving your heart and a signed contract of love and devotion. This will also hopefully gain you confidence that these guys are into you for other reasons that what you can do for them.

Finding bad dates

Dear Brent,

I know that I want to find someone for a committed relationship, but I can't seem to find anyone who is not lying, cheating or a complete freak show. I am the first to admit that I have an extremely negative attitude right now toward my ability to meet anyone decent when I go out. How do I fight off feeling so angry and keep trying to connect with that right person when I'm really not feeling driven anymore?

When attempting to form social connections, it is important to maintain a positive outlook when you go out. Your attitude about people or situations drives so many things and can be a helpful benefit or a huge barrier. Like a lactose-intolerant person that just ate a large cheese pizza, your stinky-ass negative attitude can be noticed from across the room and will definitely make people gag if they smell it. Be aware that the impression you are putting off could be repelling good people.

Another odor that can turn others off just as quickly is that cologne that so many wear called "Desperation for Men." It can be an overpowering scent that many drown themselves in. That pungent awful fragrance makes most men run in terror. It is generally sprayed generously by those exhibiting nervousness, self-loathing or other emotional shortcomings. Unfortunately, instead of covering it up, the scent often makes it even more obvious that the men who wear it are not interesting or stable.

These stinky people embody some of the most toxic qualities that can keep someone from meeting great people. Many times individuals do not identify that they are presenting these traits and may be subjecting others to negative attitudes repeatedly. It is important to start changing behaviors that are off-putting to the types of people you want to attract. The belief that "opposites attract," does not generally hold true for negative people. Many times they attract people just as damaged and grumpy as they are, leaving both parties miserable throughout their interactions.

You state that you are ready for a committed relationship. I'm sure you feel deserving of someone awesome to wake up next to in the morning that will have dinner waiting for you on the table when you get home from work and will scratch your back whenever you are itchy. In preparation for this, work on addressing some internal beliefs and frustrations about guys in the dating world so you can have a positive outlook when you go out. It will help to ensure that you will be ready, willing and able to form a positive relationship when you do eventually meet that great guy.

Internal improvements can have a significant positive impact in our external world. Check your bad attitude at the door. Re-evaluate where you are meeting people and how you pursue opportunities to get to know them. If you are dating drunks, quit trying to meet people in bars. If you find yourself dating liars, cheaters or needy people, consider taking the time to get to know them better before putting faith in them being someone that is a benefit in your life.

Beauty in balance

Dear Brent,

I know I'm not the hottest guy on the planet, but I'm not ugly either. I'm not expecting that everyone is attracted to me, but it seems like there are so many guys that are way too superficial and only looking for someone that is really hot. I have many great qualities that I think people would appreciate, but it seems like I can't even get to the initial meeting to let them get to know me. Why does it seem like you have to be gorgeous to get anywhere with dating?

There are some in our community that feel that physical beauty is much more important than what exists under the surface. Many of us may have the tendency to gauge our self-esteem by how we look in the mirror, appear to others, or how often we get flirted with when we go out or log on. Although not completely based around those activities, many times we may feel less attractive due to how we are seeing ourselves at that moment. Our self-esteem impacts our confidence and may influence our decision to engage others in conversation or flirt with a cute guy across the room. Ego blows can be devastating, especially if we are causing them from our own internal feelings. So many of us struggle with our insecurities, but they are made so much worse when we feel that we are being rejected or dismissed because of them.

On the flip side, there are also things that we find attractive in others that we search out. Some of them are directly apparent while others take a little digging to discover. There are an infinite number of qualities that individuals are attracted to, not just the ones that can be noticed during a first glance. Of course, there are other things that are noticed more quickly like physical appearance that can entice an onlooker to look harder and deeper.

Thankfully there is a wide variety of qualities that people find attractive. Fortunately for most of us, it is much more than simply six-pack abs and baby blue eyes. I think most people would agree that a hot douchebag is still a douchebag. They may be pretty looking and could assist you in a fantasy when rubbing one out, but chances are that their personality would be a huge barrier to creating any type of friendship or deeper connection.

In a perfect world, there would not be a concern about inner and outer beauty being out of balance. We would all be completely contented. I'm not proposing that the only awesome people are those that have the sex appeal of Bradley Cooper paired with the intellect of Einstein, the giving nature of Mother Theresa, and the social proclivities of Justin Timberlake. In reality, we can only work on ourselves by trying to find a healthy balance of personal aspects that makes us feel like a well-rounded person. Be careful about developing the perception that only physically attractive people get anywhere in the dating world.

Of course physical characteristics are some of the most identifiable reasons why you may be checking someone out or want to go up to strike up a conversation, but hopefully after the initial meeting happens, you have the opportunity to peel back the layers of the individual and find more engaging aspects about them. In turn, they can dive deeper into your gooey center to find out about the amazing parts of you as well. Luckily, there are fantastic people out there that will be drawn to internal and external qualities while appreciating us for who we are. They are amazing inside and outside with beautiful personalities and souls to match. This combo can make them hot as hell.

Dating younger guys

Dear Brent,

I am in my late 40s and am physically attracted to men in their early 20s. The sex is usually good, but the relationships don't last long. I am left feeling like they have taken advantage of me financially and wasted my time. How can I find a relationship with someone that makes me feel good physically and emotionally?

Your answer to finding a fulfilling relationship may lie in determining the type of person you want to date, not only because they are young pretty guys. Hopefully there are other qualities that are desirable to you, not just that a potential partner is under a particular age. Youth is often characterized by impulsivity and immaturity, but as many of us have experienced, dating older people does not necessarily guarantee stability, maturity, or wisdom. Wanting a healthy relationship is a great goal, but pursuing it with the wrong person will not produce what you want. You can have amazing sex together, but have nothing to talk about afterwards. He can be adorable, but may not share in any of your interests or hopes for the future. These differences can happen regardless of the age difference.

Relationships can exist in a variety of configurations and compositions. The players may differ in age, profession, body type, race, HIV status, and life experiences, while others seem like carbon copies of each other. Each relationship is unique and has its own set of strengths and challenges.

One problem with being attracted to a certain type of person is that you may be looking primarily for physical characteristics and placing more importance on looks and image than on the internal qualities that make you feel emotionally close to them. Just because someone can fulfill your physical desires doesn't mean they will necessarily be good for your brain or heart. So many of us get stuck in looking for someone that fits our fantasy type. Hopefully we are all turned on by the physical appearance of our partner, but fulfillment in a healthy relationship generally doesn't exist with that alone.

You mentioned being taken advantage of financially, so I am left to assume that you are paying for many of your activities and expenses. Sometimes in these situations one partner is left feeling like a "sugar daddy" even if that role has not been established directly in the relationship. If you're getting upset with the frivolous spending of your money by your boyfriend, maybe it would be a good time to evaluate how you give away this aspect of control to him. If you give this freely, then I'm not sure why you feel justified in being pissed off at him. If you allow him to choose a bottle of wine at dinner that is $175 instead of a $40 one without expressing that you feel that it is excessive, you are mostly to blame for this situation. It is possible that your boyfriend could be America's next top sommelier, but there is a better chance that he is associating the price with quality or simply enjoying buying something expensive. If he is really insistent about getting that higher priced item, you could suggest that he pays for it.

A major concern is that you may be in a habit of showing off to others or trying to purchase love. It can be a very sweet trait to do nice things for others because it makes them feel happy or they get the sense that you care about them. Some people try to counteract low self-esteem or work to solidify a relationship by attempting to impress people with money, material items, or status. A full money clip, expensive car, or name dropping does not mean that you are desirable to anyone except those who really don't care about who you really are. They may be primarily concerned about what you can provide to them. Be careful about those who primarily want to be involved with you as it relates to their benefit or can be kept in your life by the promise of gaining more from you than just your love.

Clingy men desperately searching for a relationship

Dear Brent,

I have recently become single after a four-year relationship and am enjoying my time being single. I've had some great dates and sex, but don't feel that I am ready or interested in pursuing another relationship right now. There have been a few guys that said they're ready to jump into a monogamous relationship with me after just a few dates. I've worked hard throughout my life to achieve success and feel that I'm in a good place in my life, but dealing with some of these clingy gay men is beginning to wear on me. How do I continue to actively date without the frustration of having to fight off these guys that want to date me exclusively?

Dating without some aspect of frustration probably won't happen. By putting ourselves out there, we risk awkward social situations, lame sexual encounters, maladjusted people, and catty comments from supposed friends. There are definitely some realities to keep in mind and techniques that can be used to hopefully lessen your frustration

Some people go on dates for the enjoyment of meeting new people or sharing a nice meal, while others feel that they are happiest when they are dating someone or hate to be single. There are other people that are looking for someone to supplement lacking elements within them. There are also people that are in a consistent search of their next future ex-husband when they find themselves single. Some people look at being in a relationship as validation that they are good enough, sexy enough, and gosh darn it, somebody loves them.

There is nothing wrong with looking for someone that makes our heart, brain and crotch excited. Sometimes these people turn into partners, but there is also nothing wrong with looking for someone that makes parts of us eager for one night of cuddles or a few dates. Be honest about your interests and intentions with dating. Even if he chooses to ignore your comments about only wanting to meet new people without getting into an instant relationship, at least you have done your part to put it out on the table. What others choose to do with your information is up to them.

You don't have to put the smack down on the date by stating your personal boundaries, expectations, and all the crap you've experienced lately regarding exasperating dates. It could definitely ruin the mood and you are going to come across as bitter and bitchy. You can choose to just go out and have a good time. During the course of your date, you can find more tactful ways of discussing what you are looking for and your personal limits regarding relationships at this time in your life.

Don't stop being yourself just because some men respond by getting a little obsessive or energetically pursue you. Some people may misinterpret your acts of kindness and charming personality. Sometimes breakfast in bed after a night of rockin' sex can just be a sweet gesture of gratitude, expressing an interest in doing it again, or reflective of just being really hungry and not wanting to get dressed to grab a bite. Just be careful to make sure that you have done your part to ensure that your message has been sufficiently conveyed to them.

Rapid relationships

Some seem to have a consistent flow of relationships that come on strong, envelop their world, and then crash to a fiery death just as quickly as they formed. Facebook posts are created soon after a series of initial dates with some vague post about how amazing life can be. The comments begin to flow about how much they have fallen in love and are laying on the couch currently watching how cute their new guy looks while he drools on a pillow and snores. Many times these only go on for a few weeks or months before this wonderment magically transforms into devastation and we get to experience the onslaught of angry or self-loathing comments about this individual, people in the community, and relationships in general. Of course, these negative feelings can be completely resolved by the introduction of the next absolutely wonderful person that flips their world back to being a beautiful place full of wonderment and glittery unicorns prancing through fields of daffodils.

These exchanges can be frustrating to the people involved as well as those around the situation. I think it is important to take the time and effort to develop a strong foundation before people jump into a volatile two-week dramatic relationship that will soon lead into homicidal feelings and make people want to unfriend you on Facebook because of your tragic posts. First of all, public displays of disaster are so much more uncomfortable than public displays of affection, whether it be online or in a bar. Second, many experience the "honeymoon period" where people appear perfect and conflict seems to be the furthest thing from a possibility. Of course this is not a realistic expectation for any relationships. Until the point where you have taken the opportunity to truly get to know someone, deciding to date them may not be a good decision. Rushing into this may bite you in the ass and cause high degrees of frustration later. You are going to have to look deeper than if they have a nice butt, killer smile, or can hump like a porn star. Don't attempt to overlook someone's negative or concerning behaviors just because you want to get laid or feel that they are going to be just good enough to date. These issues will most likely continue to re-surface and cause you to become extremely frustrated throughout your time together.

Sometimes relationships appear to be a beautiful exchange of passion that will seemingly never end. Over a short period of time however, some promises made become less likely to ever be fulfilled and the participants are left wondering what happened to all those sweet words and wonderful intentions. It's possible that interest simply faded or someone was taken for a ride. Maybe they haven't spent the time to get to know each other well enough or have not adequately expressed their hopes and expectations for the relationship. Of course, actions speak much louder than words most times. When people don't follow through or perform in contrary ways to how they promise to act, we are left feeling disappointed or angry. There are also times where these situations may become uncomfortable or abusive, sometimes so subtly we don't even recognize that our relationships are slipping into dangerous territories.

There are many potential reasons for these types of relationships to form. Some people may become somewhat "addicted" to the newness of an initial relationship or see these situations as a means to get what they want. Maybe they are experiencing a desire to fulfill some fantasy they think will significantly improve their lives. It is important to take a step back and look at why you are enamored with someone. Be cautious of impulsive decisions. Although not always the case, these situations have a tendency to end poorly for all parties involved. This does not have to happen. Although it takes work, spend time getting to know your potential partner on deeper levels than just having fun and experiencing the excitement of a new relationship. It can help to ensure more long-term success.

Searching for the wrong soul mate

Many times we are looking for a boyfriend, partner, husband, someone to date, or just a consistent person to hang out and have sex with that is less of a defined committed relationship, but more than a passing fancy. Of course we want that person that makes our eyes bug out and groin pulse with anxious excitement. It's unfortunate that many times when this happens, the physical amazement isn't enough to forge a lasting exciting relationship and our interest can quickly fade.

If you are looking to causally date, then a high level of compatibility doesn't necessarily need to be there. You can focus on physical attraction and enjoyment of activities, while philosophical beliefs and childhood traumas don't matter as much. When someone is truly looking for a person for exploration into a deeper relationship, there are infinitely more factors that are even more important to assess than physical attractiveness and enjoyment of social activities.

Of course, we generally begin our search by looking for someone that is attractive to us. There is nothing wrong with desiring a good-looking person, but this may be one of the most significant stumbling blocks in finding a great guy. Strangely enough, some of the most fulfilling and long-lasting relationships may not be with the spitting image of the person you imagined in your daydream fantasies. Much of relationship compatibility comes from a variety of other aspects. It's because of this truth that one of the biggest factors of online matchmaking is pairing profiles based on analyzing multiple compatibilities including beliefs, interests, perceptions, filthy activities, and life goals.

I understand that there has to be something that initially attracts you to that person. In truth, physical qualities are usually some of the first things that smacks us across the face. But much like any advertisement, the visual component can be appealing, but the quality, taste, smell, consistency, availability, and satisfaction of that product will dictate if we are motivated to keep coming back for more.

Being intrigued by someone is so much more than being interested in a few surface things about them. There are quirks and neurotic behaviors that each of us possess that make us strange and unique. We all have issues and challenges that have hurt or empowered us. As far as our past, remember it is important to have complimentary baggage, but it doesn't need to match. Having many of the same concerns doesn't necessarily help a relationship grow and flourish. It is also important to try to identify someone's idiosyncrasies and patterns that are intriguing, challenging, frustrating, and adorable. It is absolutely crucial to have effective and healthy communication to navigate difficulties between people. Although it doesn't always assure a positive outcome in a conflict, it definitely doesn't hurt when both people use their effective skills together.

There is so much intricacy in relationships with other people and each comes with their own set of complexities. We need to get past the superficial beauty of someone to find out if there is true compatibility. Take some time to dive inside and snoop around if you really want to get to know someone. The outer layer is the easiest to fake and the inside is the most important to love if you are going to find that wonderful relationship.

It is also important to get into a relationship that compliments you as a person, not completes you. If you feel like an incomplete person, then work on filling yourself up with success and confidence instead of using a relationship with someone else to plug your self-confidence void. Insecurity will tear apart relationships quickly and lead people into situations for the wrong reasons. There is a huge difference between "good" and "good enough." If you are on a primary hunt to find a partner, you may be willing to settle for less than you should. Being open to finding a boyfriend is a great mindset to experience, but if it leads into desperation while searching, you may end up with the wrong type of person.

That amazing relationship can be around the corner, but be careful about glossing over someone that could be a fantastic person in your life. Don't get overly fixated on what Prince Studly will look like. Be focused on finding someone worthy of being in your life and fulfilling to be around.

Shying away from emotional connections

Relationships come in many forms. Not everyone is

looking for a husband, but the "blow-and-go" can become quite unfulfilling. For many, hooking up for sex is easy, but the hard part is finding people that really enjoy spending time hanging out or snuggling on the couch. There are many things to love about sex, but most of us crave a connected encounter beyond just screwing around. It makes me concerned that a large chunk of our population has significant challenges forming emotional connections or showing affection. Instead of working on becoming closer together, we may be disconnecting further from each other.

Of course there are truly different strokes for different folks, sometimes quite literally. For many, sexual contact is an extremely intimate activity while others consider it more of an activity similar to going to the store or putting gas in your car. It's something that you do to fulfill a need when it arises and then you simply move on to the next task at hand. Some feel that sex with someone can be fine once, but after that initial excitement is gone, then the encounter doesn't need to be repeated. It is totally understandable to not go back for a second helping of a dish that isn't tasty, but if it is a yummy choice, I'm not sure why someone would not want to stick it in their mouth again. Getting caught in a spiral of constantly searching for new sexual encounters can be exhausting, but also signals concerns about the desire to continue engaging in single-session meetings. It may help to fine tune your sexual skills with lots of practice, but not to build any form of connection with others except during that limited amount of interaction.

The "you can totally pound my ass, but don't kiss me" mentality does exist out there. Some shy away from taking the time to chat so you can get to know each other. Sex where you cuddle afterward is an alien concept for others. It seems like it is easier at times to find someone for a 20-minute roll in the hay than it is to find a cool guy for a movie and snuggle. Some feel that intercourse is the most intimate encounter while others feel it's something you do to get your rocks off. Looking people in the eye while kissing them can be considered too over the top and awkward while others really get off on it.

For some, showing emotional connection can be difficult, uncomfortable, or scary. People may have experienced negative situations in the past with their family, friends, or past relationships that have caused them to build walls around them to protect their sensitive parts from getting hurt. Certain topics, activities, and feelings terrify people due to the extreme personal nature of what it can bring up for them. For some, physically sexual things may be totally acceptable while emotional aspects of actions will cause them to avoid the interaction or run away from this perceived "intimate" and threatening encounter.

Technology is often blamed for our lack of emotional connection due to reliance on things like phone apps and web-based tools for communication. Unfortunately these may cause feelings more akin to shopping on Amazon rather than looking to make a connection. We are looking for that impulse item that we cannot live without, even though we just saw it for the first time. It peaks our interest for a short time, but won't last long after the excitement has worn off. It will be discarded for the next bright and shiny object of affection.

There is nothing wrong with having casual sexual contacts, but it is ultimately important that all parties involved are on similar pages regarding what each person expects and desires. Being upfront about your intentions and those things you want can help you ensure that your encounters are positive ones. If you're not going to get what you really want, then don't do it. Don't let being horny lead you into having encounters that leave you feeling unfulfilled and lonely. If you're that worked up, take matters into your own hands and don't waste time with other people. Save the naked time to be shared with someone else that will be interested in getting to know you, being truly intimate, and may actually be up for second round.

Effeminate male searching to be butch

Dear Brent,

I've been on a few dates with a guy who told me that he isn't usually into effeminate guys, but I'm the "exception." I was offended because I never thought of myself as effeminate. I believe I show an average amount of "masculinity" as a regular person. When I expressed my feelings to him, he just said I was being dramatic and that was proof that I'm more like a woman. I started asking some friends about how they saw me and a couple of them agreed I do have some effeminate qualities. I feel that my self-image is shattered. I'm not really attracted to effeminate men either. I feel like I need to throw out all my clothes, lift weights, and arrange for friends to slap me every time I sound too queeny.

This brings up a very concrete memory for me. In the movie "In & Out," Kevin Cline's character attempts to butch it up using a self-help tape. At the end of the day, he had to be honest about himself in many ways, including accepting the fact that he was not going to be the epitome of a rugged country guy and that accepting himself was the right thing to do for him. All of us have to develop our personal identities including what career path suites our interests, the friends we want, and who we choose to date. As gay men, we are also challenged to figure out what clothes to wear, where to tear it up on Saturday night, and how many times we use the word "girl" or "gurl" or " gggguuuuuurrrrrrrrrl" throughout the day.

There are so many phrases in our society that hurt people as they try to figure out their identity. Early on, we may have been told to "man up" or that "quit acting like a little girl." We can then get hooked on using phrases like "butch" and "straight-acting." Words can be used to describe beautiful images or destroy self-esteem.

I'm challenging myself to think of what defines masculine and feminine qualities and wondering what your friends are noticing in you that they are considering "effeminate." I don't think that people act like a woman if you tear up during a touching part of a movie. I would be more concerned if a "masculine" person feels like they can't cry when something moves them. Unfortunately, some of these antiquated and judgmental views can impact people in very negative ways, including increasing feelings of depression, isolation, and discrimination. As far as acting like a woman, my Mom is female and I think she kicks ass.

You mentioned wanting to change your outward appearance by getting your body muscled and dressing more butch. Keep in mind that just because a guy has bulging biceps, a leather vest, and rides a motorcycle doesn't mean that he doesn't have the potential to queen-out and talk about fashion, candle-making, or meatloaf recipes. Your outward appearance is simply one aspect of you that people see. Hopefully it is not the most important or impressive part of who you are. If it is, then you may want to take some time and figure out what you really like about yourself and what makes you attractive, desirable, and unique.

If your personal style is going to be impacted by who you want to date, then be prepared to knock down a few walls in your home to build extra closet space for your various wardrobes. You can have sections for cowboy, dance club, leather, twink, and opera drag just to cover your bases in case a cute guy from one of these scenes hits on you. Oh yeah, don't forget about a wide selection of hats, gloves, and shoes. That's very important to put on an accurate impression to someone else so you can fit in.

Fortunately life doesn't have to be about fitting in to one particular image. Be careful about changing yourself for anyone other than yourself. If your self-esteem is going to be based on other's impressions of you, then you are in for a life of trying to please everyone else and figuring out ways to get them to like you. Consider the scene in "Birdcage" where Nathan Lane is trying to learn to be more butch. Take a lesson from him and work on becoming less worried about piercing the toast and more concerned about what flavor of jelly you really enjoy. Don't focus on how your buddies tell you to smear. It truly doesn't matter if you define yourself as butch, fem, queeny, or rugged. The most important thing is that you like and appreciate yourself. Don't forget, most of these qualities are totally subjective anyway. To paraphrase from one of my dearest friends, "I don't care how straight-acting you say you are, you still look really gay when you're on your knees sucking me."

Gay racial discrimination

Dear Brent,

I am an African-American gay man. I have a very good job, nice car and home, workout three times a week, and love to travel. My problem is that I can't find a man in my life. I am attracted to straight or bisexual white or Latin men. Many white guys in town don't like black guys or other men of color. I know some are secretly attracted to other races and they don't want their friends to know. Guys seem to be shallow and more interested in the color of your skin than your personality. What should I do to find someone to date?

Unfortunately when we are not getting the response and attention we want from others, it is easy to become jaded, bitter, and grumpy. There are very few absolutes in the world. Hopefully some gay men in the city are interested in guys from a variety of racial and ethnic backgrounds and would embrace those from a variety of body types, social groups, and interests. It would be a shame if white dudes were the only ones getting laid or having relationships.

Having said that, we are all attracted to certain types of people and qualities they possess. Sometimes when someone makes our bunny jump, it is strictly physical, while other times a fantastic sense of humor, razor-sharp intellect, or love of traveling can provide a strong attraction for someone. Identifying what is interesting to us when interacting with others is an important part of accepting ourselves.

Be careful not to generalize that gay men in your city discriminate against black guys, unless you live in an area where some terribly outdated racial beliefs exist. Hopefully this is not the case, but if it is, you may want to consider relocating to a more progressive city if your desire is to date open-minded guys.

It's normal to be turned down for some reason, be it our ethnicity, body type, HIV status, height, hobbies, sexual interests, or having hair on our backs. We have all been turned down by someone for something. We have also most likely turned someone down that doesn't interest us. No one is attractive to everyone. So getting turned down should not completely destroy our self-esteem. When we develop a bad attitude about meeting people, hooking up, or going on dates, we risk limiting ourselves from taking chances to potentially meet some amazing new people. Be careful about letting a negative outlook keep you from connecting with others.

Here are a few other thoughts relating to your letter. It seems that you take some pride in certain accomplishments in your life. I find it interesting that you talk about people being interested in only surface aspects of a person's race, but surface qualities are what you focused on in your letter about you and then to describe the person you want to meet using only similar surface qualities. You discussed your profession, possessions and interests, but not other important qualities like having a great sense of humor or talent for cooking.

You then identified being attracted to men only from two ethnic backgrounds with two options for their sexual orientation, bisexual or straight. I'm assuming that you might dismiss a gay Arab guy since he does not fit into your general definition of attractive people. Not only are all of these desired traits based on surface characteristics, but you do not express other qualities of substance that are important to you to find in someone else.

Another interesting aspect of your concern is that you are going after people of two sexual orientations that would have a low chance of being committed or fulfilled in a relationship with you regardless of your race. A bisexual male might not be completely fulfilled with only a relationship with a male or may be struggling with his sexuality as he takes a slow train to Gayville. A "straight" man that is with you is first of all not "straight," but also most likely cheating on someone or on the down-low from people in his life.

I'm also concerned by your comment that guys are embarrassed to admit to their friends that they are attracted to a man of color. To me that just seems extremely judgmental and bitchy. This may be your own way of coping with feelings of loneliness and frustration when attempting to date, but be careful about putting these emotions on other people around you.

Take some time to think about what is going on internally with you. It seems that maintaining some of these ideas and attitudes may be keeping you in a negative headspace and from having to have a healthy relationship with a man. In ideal situations, we find ourselves attracted to physically and emotionally beautiful and available people that make our head, heart, and groins jump up and down in excitement. I would first suggest taking some time to figure out what you really feel would fulfill you in a dating situation and then go out looking for it.

Of preferences or prejudice

I hear many people talking about how the gay scene is full of discrimination. Many times this relates to when people are talking about why someone doesn't want to go on a date with them or isn't interested in a sweaty sexual encounter. Since words are extremely important and powerful in their function to describe our world, I think it is vital to use accurate words to describe situations.

Discrimination is based around the idea of excluding or looking down at an individual based on their appearance or having a preconceived idea of who they are or how they will act. It focuses on putting down individuals or groups to make them feel that others possess some power or superiority over them. Having preferences however speaks to a person's desire to be interested in some things while feeling disinterested in others. The claim that someone is discriminatory is a strong one. It accuses the person of a character defect. This means that there is something wrong with them due to incorrect or misguided thinking or that potentially they feel they are better than someone else.

There are so many reasons why people are attracted to each other. A person's physical build, height, skin tone, eye color, social style, dick size, flair for fashion, or an ultra-modern hair style can draw people together. There are also a variety of differences about how we spend our time, the music we enjoy, how we worship, and the amount of alcohol we drink when we go out. Additionally, there are other aspects of us that may attract some and disinterest others. These may include our ethnicity, body fat percentage, HIV status, how we socialize, number of tattoos, profession, relationship status, and sexual interests.

The fact that we have our own set of preferences does not necessarily mean that we are closed-minded or inappropriately judge others. We should take the time and energy to figure out who and what turns us on and embrace those things. Many times when people cry discrimination, they may more accurately be describing feeling angry or upset that they do not fit the mold of someone's preference. We have all turned someone down for one reason or another in addition to be turned down ourselves. This is not necessarily due to being discriminatory, sexist, racist, HIV-phobic, or judgmental. It is most likely due to not being what someone is looking for in general or at that specific moment.

This does not necessarily need to be considered discrimination. I don't feel that I am being inappropriately "discriminatory" against females since my sexual orientation drives by desires to get naked and sweaty with only men. I'm not a woman hater or female-phobic. I'm simply gay. That being said, I do have interests in particular types of men. There are a variety of things that intrigue and interest me about my partners, both physically and emotionally. I'm not exactly sure where these interests are with every person I encounter, but I definitely know when someone or something does or doesn't turn me on.

I don't think anyone would argue that I need to engage with every person that comes into my field of vision. None of us have that much available time in our lives. We all have the ability to choose. Our dating and sex life is not an equal opportunity employer or bound by the rules of relationship affirmative action. Although it may kick our self-esteem in a tender place, I think it is perfectly fine to not be interested in spending time with someone for a variety of reasons. You don't necessarily have to give a full dissertation about all of the reasons why you aren't interested, but having compassion for someone's feelings is really important.

Of course there is a flip side to this discussion. It is important to also be aware of not jumping to quick conclusions about someone or judging a book only by its cover. We may have the potential to make snap decisions and not give people chances if they do not initially appear to be what we think we want. Getting to know people is a great way to see if there is potential for deeper connections beyond what you may notice superficially. If you're interested in spending time with a person or not, I would hope that we all interact with each other with respect and kindness regardless if you're interested in dating or sexual contact with them.

The humane turn down

Dear Brent,

What are the best ways to turn someone down? People have told me that they aren't interested in hanging out with me in nice ways and those that were really mean. I don't want to be a jerk, but there are just some guys that hit on me that I'm not interested in. Sometimes they pick up on my hints, but other guys seem oblivious and keep on pursuing me. I've never found a comfortable way to turn them down that doesn't make me feel badly that I've possibly hurt their feelings.

I think it's really great that there are still some people out there that are concerned about other people's emotional wellbeing. One of the first words most of us learn when we are young children is "no," but when it comes to expressing this kind of disinterest about someone, it has the potential to bring up some emotional issues on both ends. I don't think many of us enjoy turning people down or not getting what we want by others turning us down.

So, the simple answer to your question would be to just say "thank you, but I'm really not interested." Of course it is not that simple. Turning someone down not only involves your concerns about how the other person takes it, but what it may bring up within us. We could evaluate why we feel the way we do, but we can also look at if declining someone's advances can bring up feelings of rejection from the past. We may have some self-esteem issues or recollections of bad situations that continue to live in our memories and are awakened through situations like these.

Turning someone down may be further complicated when the person you're interacting with has trouble with rejection, potentially causing a self-loathing, aggressive or abusive response. They may not only feel that their proposition is being rejected, but also feel rejected as a person. This emotional baggage exists inside many of us and has the potential to cause some very strong responses when triggered. Unfortunately there are also some people that choose to hear what they want to hear and ignore the words that come out of your mouth. These people continue to attempt to engage us in ways that make us feel uncomfortable or angry.

Some good general suggestions to keep in mind when you are making the decision to turn someone down is to remain as polite as possible while standing firm to your boundaries. Be careful of sending mixed signals when you are trying to turn someone down in a nice way. Sometimes beating around the bush or not being direct enough to lower the impact of hurt feelings can be confusing for them or not get your message across correctly. You may want to be a sweet person, but saying no and then continuing to engage them in ways that may show them hope in future interactions only keeps them coming back for more. There are times where your perception of being nice could be translated into potential interest in them. Of course, their perceptions may also be tainted by an overwhelming desire to be close to you.

In addition to being thoughtful about someone's feelings, you may also want to be honest with them about what makes you disinterested. It may be that you do not want to date anyone or more specifically you don't want to date them. There are also times where maybe you don't want to be that specific and just want to get out of the situation. There may be some extremely good reasons why they are not a good match for you, but helping them identify some character concerns you perceive may assist them in addressing them, thus helping them become more aware of how they come across to others.

As much as it can suck to be turned down, it's good to know you're barking up the wrong tree as soon as possible. Wasting time is a total bummer too. None of us enjoy rejection, but it is helpful to be prepared when it comes up and at least you can be nice about it. Hopefully others are as thoughtful when turning us down.

Games make the world go round

CAUTION: THIS NEXT COLUMN IS SIMPLY A PARODY. MANIPULATING OTHERS FOR YOUR OWN BENEFIT COULD RESULT IN LOSING THE FEW PEOPLE IN YOUR LIFE THAT MAY ACTUALLY BE THERE FOR YOU WHEN THINGS GET ROUGH.

Dear Brent,

I don't understand the games that so many gay men seem to play. I want to meet some interesting guys for an occasional date or sex, but it is really difficult most of the time. So many of them want to chat endlessly online and if you can actually get them to commit to meeting, often they don't follow through or disappear completely without explanation. I'm getting really frustrated with the state of our scene and wonder why I keep trying to make it work.

Some people feel that our gay culture is plagued with people playing games. It sounds like you just need to get better at playing it. We often find the game difficult to play and seemingly more impossible to win. That's most likely because we don't understand the rules. Running after people to connect with them emotionally, intellectually, or physically is at the core of why we keep trying. The thrill of the chase may only prove successful five percent of the time, but that is what makes it so damn sweet when it does.

Think about any situation where the payoff doesn't happen every time. Gambling would not be as exciting if you won $1,000 each time you pulled the slot machine handle. It is so much more fulfilling when you win after pulling the lever hundreds of times and investing a big wad of money before you get that amazing sound of falling coins and an ear-piercing alarm. The desperation and frustration you feel after so many times of trying and trying to make something happen can be alleviated by just one success. It doesn't matter how long it takes or how much time or effort you invest. As long as you can get an occasional success, it is totally worth it.

There are many people out there that must ascribe to this philosophy. They make us work hard to meet up. That sweet, sweet payoff is so much more fulfilling because we don't get what we want all the time. They are helping us build up that desire to give us that huge release when we finally get in front of that person. It's what makes these exchanges exciting and worthwhile. In many ways, playing this seemingly unwinnable game of attempted connecting actually benefits us in the long run by teaching us patience and that we will not always be a winner. Learning how to lose gracefully is a really important skill to learn.

Be cautious of complaining that things don't happen on your time-frame. We can't always get what we want as soon as we want it. Connecting with others isn't like going to a fast-food restaurant. Your impatience with these situations and feelings of entitlement that people need to fulfill your every desire can be considered truly undesirable traits that may be one of the primary reasons why people may not want to follow through with you. People generally don't like those who are self-centered and have unrealistic expectations, especially those who dictate that people need to follow through with their promises. It may be time to re-evaluate how important you think you are and how valuable your time is. Common sense and common courtesy should not be expected.

One final thought on the topic. You may want to consider that it is usually more fulfilling not to meet in person anyway. So many times people are much more interesting online than they could ever hope to be in person. If they don't know the answer to a question, they can look it up. If they don't like themselves, they can work on creating a persona that incorporates the charm of Channing Tatum, the wit of John Stewart, and the filthy talk of Titan porn star Dirk Caber. Trust me, fiction is most times so much better than factual reality, especially with people in our community.

Develop your inner douchebag

BEWARE: THIS COLUMN IS SIMPLY A SATIRE OF SITUATIONS AND PEOPLE MANY OF US FACE ON A REGULAR BASIS. DO NOT TRY THESE AT HOME, IN A BAR, OR ANYWHERE ELSE UNLESS YOU WANT THE POTENTIAL FOR SOME NASTY REPERCUSSIONS.

I have been writing these columns with the primary purpose of helping people create better, more fulfilling lives. In light of the overwhelming patterns emerging in our culture around people acting in thoughtless, judgmental, and mean-spirited ways, this tutorial will help you become better equipped to deal with these types of situations and people. Don't worry about trying to change other people's behaviors or have your own integrity by acting like a nice guy. It's better to just give in, fit in, and act like a douchebag. Everyone else seems to be doing it, so follow along. Focus on trying these out throughout your interactions. Don't forget that practice makes perfect! Hopefully you get really good at these techniques. If you need some assistance, feel free to get a coach. There are plenty of experts out there.

Make six dates for the same day and time just in case people flake out.

If nothing else, you can be well positioned for an orgy or a small dinner party if everyone shows up. You have to cover your bases since everyone else will be looking for other opportunities and making multiple plans as well since so many people fail to show up or follow through.

Ask whatever personal questions you want.

It's best to have initial conversations discussing the size of their equipment, favorite sexual activities, or requesting pictures of them screwing, especially before you know other things about them. Get these most important questions out in the open and answered upfront. Learning about other aspects, interests, motivations, and strengths most likely prove to be a boring conversation anyway. Regardless, people are rarely worth more than just a sexy romp.

Don't bother showing up or let someone know you won't be coming after making concrete plans with them.

It takes way too long to shoot a thoughtful note like a quick text message so they can do something else instead of waiting for you. Don't worry, your time is definitely more precious than theirs and they probably wouldn't be doing anything else more productive with their time anyway.

Don't worry about treating someone badly.

If someone contacts you and you're not interested, put them in their place and tell them about why you would never think about meeting up with them by pointing out that you think they are ugly or a loser. It's much better to do something like this than risk saying thank you and having them continue to pursue you. Stop them in their tracks before they have the ability to waste your time with further messages. Hopefully being mean to them will get them to either leave social networking sites or quit trying to meet people. Those who reach out to people who are out of their league need to be reminded that there are consequences to sending unsolicited messages.

If you're not attractive, find pictures of someone that you think will lure someone into meeting you.

Don't worry if you don't really look like that picture. The other person will probably be so desperate that it won't matter. Most of us just want to get off and it doesn't really matter who it is with. If necessary, burying a face in a pillow is always a great option.

Practice snarky comments, aggressive body language, and bitchy facial expressions to keep people away.

The only people that you will attract will be those awesome guys that are playing the same game and will notice what you are doing. If you look kind and approachable, undesirable people will see you as an easy target. It's better to put up those walls so you don't have to deal with lame guys.

Keep looking for a better option after you make firm plans with someone.

Trust me, there are tons of hotter people just around the corner. Don't quit the search because it will be worth it when some other stud shows up to fulfill your fantasies better than the earlier one. You won't be happy until you have the hottest guy and shouldn't have to settle unless you have exhausted all potential options. Keep looking for that perfect choice and never settle for what you would consider second best.

Hot and heavy conversations should leave them wanting more.

Don't ruin it by giving them anything physical from you. If you tell them that you are truly interested in meeting, they will keep pumping you with hot masturbation material that you will never have to do in person. Heavy flirting and sexy talk is a great way to keep them hooked without having to put the effort into what could happen in person.

Refuse to open the door when someone shows up to mess around.

The thrill of the chase is so awesome, even more exciting than the act itself. It should be satisfying enough to know you made them want you and that they are leaving angry and sexually frustrated.

Do whatever you can to get off without reciprocation for your partner.

If they don't get off before you, then that's their problem. After shooting, either jump up to wipe off before putting on your pants or roll over to fall asleep. They can pleasure themselves. It's more important that we get our own needs met.

CHAPTER 2: ONLINE & TECHNOLOGY

Wasting time online

Dear Brent,

My patience is quickly running out with being online. I have wasted so much time trying to connect with people and have gotten burned often. There are times where it seems like conversations are going well and then it goes nowhere. I thought online and mobile dating opportunities were supposed to help people meet each other, but I feel more alone and disconnected than I think I was before everyone was online. What am I doing wrong or are websites just a really bad place to meet good people?

My general philosophy is that you can meet amazing people almost anywhere, even online. Keep in mind that effective online conversations should help to get you offline and out enjoying life. So many express frustrations about being online and the general lack of success in connecting with others. The cyber-social culture is such a large part of our community and can be a very complicated environment to navigate successfully for many people. It can definitely be used effectively for meeting friends, making dates, or hooking up.

But there are a wide range of elements, techniques, and

45

concerns to address regarding how to successfully navigate these muddy waters. Like many things we experience in our lives, tools are not positive or negative. They should be defined by the way they can be used to benefit us and to help create the outcomes we want. An online presence is like this as well. It can possess many aspects that are either beneficial or frustrating to us as individuals and as a community. There are great potential outcomes that can happen when communicating online. You can talk to a gorgeous, charismatic doctor from Berlin or have a webcam session with a muscle guy from Miami. These situations may not have been otherwise possible depending on where you live or how much money you have to travel. These people may not live in the same city, go to the same places, or have mutual friends in common with you, but your interaction can provide something meaningful or fun. Unfortunately, many times this potential does not translate well into the real world in getting dates if the people are geographically undesirable.

It doesn't matter if a website is geared towards social marketing, specific interests, or hooking up. The only promise that any of these sites hold is the potential of helping people connect. You can find love or friendship on a hookup site or get laid from a connection you made on a social networking site. You never know who you may find out there, but here are some things to keep in mind that can increase your chances of meeting someone awesome and protect yourself from pitfalls.

It is extremely important to maintain a positive attitude when it comes to dating and being online is no exception. If you're not enjoying it, you may feel like it is a big waste of time. These negative attitudes are most likely extremely detrimental to your success. Feeling grumpy, bitter, self-loathing, aggressive, or desperate will probably be communicated in some way to others and give you the same low success rate as if you did it physically in front of someone.

As with any attempt to connect with another person, there

are opportunities for potential rejection or disappointment, but there is also the potential to meet some amazing people. You may actually find someone of quality for companionship, hot sex, or dating. There is no limit to the possibilities that can be found. Don't shoot down a method of finding someone great just because you are bitter about past experiences. Continue looking for those things in your life that make you feel great.

You can also take some time and evaluate what you have done previously and how you can try different methods in the future. Don't keep trying the same unsuccessful tactics and then complain about how people still suck. There are always opportunities to change and improve your skills when it comes to connecting with people in-person or online. You have the ability to create more effective profiles, have better exchanges, and gain more confidence. Cyberspace doesn't have to be an unhappy place.

Online games and authenticity

Dear Brent,

I am really not finding the people online that I want to connect with. I am on multiple hookup and dating sites and when I find someone that I am attracted to, they don't seem interested and rarely talk to me. Unfortunately the creepy ones seem to always send me messages. How can I become better at the online game and make my profiles more appealing to the right people?

The feeling that being online is like playing a game is quite accurate. Many people believe they never win and often also feel like a big loser. The reality is that there are rules and strategies that are helpful to know when you play any game to help you perform better and improve your chances of possibly winning.

The first thing is to figure out why you are playing this

game in the first place. Consider if you're looking for buddies, hookups, dating partners, or a fun combination of all of those. There are many benefits of using profiles to meet great people, but what you put out in cyberspace should be reflective of what you want. Take the time to figure out what parts of you are important for others to know so they can get to know you. There are so many ways to present yourself in an online profile. Think of it as a precursor to a job interview as you take a quick ride in an elevator. You only have a few moments to put out that you are an interesting candidate to fill their available slot. An insecure or pompous candidate definitely does not look impressive in this process. Think about what impression you want to put out.

One of the coolest aspects of online profiles is that you have the freedom to state exactly what you want and who you are. If you are into 6-foot tall Asian men who are packing more than 10 inches, appreciate the finer points of 18th Century chamber music, and is an expert in French cooking, say it. You can also list your strengths, interests, passions, and boundaries that you feel are important to you personally and you value in others. Like with most significant things in your life, statements in your profile should be prioritized. Figure out which qualities and desires are most important to you while some of the minor ones could be excluded.

If you have no idea of who you are, what you want, or what you're looking for in someone else, log off immediately and spend some time getting to know yourself. This will help you figure out what you want to include in your profile. Have confidence that the right people will be interested in getting to know you. There are people that actually look at your profile and read the information you have so carefully written. Make it accurate and interesting so quality people will have an opportunity to be enticed by your presentation of yourself.

Although ideas you convey in your profile give someone an extremely important first look into who you are, most times there is a visual interest that precedes reading your profile. Physical attractions can happen first, but having a good online profile adds an additional step of personal information that can be shared between people before you have a first conversation. Good photos are so important. They can show a variety of interests and personality characteristics, as well as showing your body, pretty eyes, or heart-melting smile. At times, they may be a more accurate representation of someone than their words or meant to create a false image. You may want to consider what activities you share or how much enjoyment you are showing in these pictures. Also consider being cautious about putting out naked images that can be passed around to other people or may compromise your integrity or safety.

One of the best techniques to improve your online profiles is to have a good friend give some honest feedback about your pictures and chosen words. You need to solicit impressions from people that will be honest with you. This may include feedback that they think your pants are too tight or that orange is a really bad color for you. They may have some fantastic suggestions about how to improve your profile and make it zippier. Be open to hearing their perspectives, but know that at the end of day it is your profile and you have to own it. Use it as an additional method to meet people to share your enjoyment of life.

Get off while using online social networking

Dear Brent,

These dating and hookup websites and phone applications never work. I see some people who can sometimes get laid or occasionally meet someone that seems interesting, but most of them turn out to be liars or losers. I waste so much time trying to get to meet up with people. I guess this is more of a rant than a question, but I am really frustrated that this is one of the only methods to try to connect with people outside of going to a bar or club. What do I do to fight off my feelings of just wanting to give up on meeting people?

We spend hours searching, clicking, woofing, flirting, disclosing, and sending pictures of our dogs, sushi dinners, throbbing cock shots, or a winking pucker. By the end of this process, many of us continue to feel isolated, frustrated, angry, and depressed. Unfortunately this appears to be somewhat of the norm when using these technological methods.

We continue to beat our heads against this cyber wall hoping that this tech culture will spontaneously change and begin working for us. People will be interested in meeting up in-person, not disappear when we make plans, and be honest about their intentions. They will look like their pictures, be easy to carry on an interesting conversation, and remember to chomp on a breath mint before getting close to us. As we have hopefully figured out, it is going to take much more than wishing, hoping, thinking, and praying.

Instead of simply desiring these changes, let's agree to start working on adjusting our own methods about how we use these tools to connect with others. The only time things change is if we put the effort into changing them. It needs to start with ourselves. When we create change in our own lives to do things differently, it can influence others to create similar changes, especially if they see how modifying old methods and behaviors can be more effective. If enough people jump on, we begin to have an impact in our community at large.

Effective use of technology has the ability to connect us with people that we may not have the opportunity to chat with otherwise. I challenge each of you who use technology to support your social life and work on using these tools for what they were designed for, which is to provide an initial introduction to someone. It is the fault of the end users if potential relationships get locked away in the cyberspace void.

Quit blaming the tool.

If someone resists breaking out of a technology-facilitated conversation, then it is up to you to move on and put your energies into someone that is more in alignment with your interests, goals, and desires. With all the people out there who complain about the games and frustrations online paired with a desire for face-to-face contact, I'm sure you can find at least a few of those who share the same desires to log off. Focus on them to help alleviate some of your frustrations.

I believe that one individual can make a difference. Stand up against this flagrant misuse of potentially amazing methods of meeting people. Stop being technology's little bitch! For God's sake, if you have a good chat going with someone, make plans to meet up and do something away from the glow of a computer screen or your smart phone. Once a connection is made, log off from those sites and applications so you can enjoy the person that is also interested in connecting in the real world. Trust me, getting off online chats as soon as possible increases your changes for you to get off in other much more enjoyable ways.

The right tool for the right job

Dear Brent,

I am so sick of all of these websites and smartphone applications that are supposed to help people connect for sex or relationships. I'm tired of wasting my time since I only find people that aren't looking for real ways to connect. I wasn't successful before these became popular, and I'm definitely not any closer to finding a boyfriend after using these either.

I hear these kinds of comments all the time. Strangely enough, there are some people that are extremely successful in getting what they want by using technology, but more times than not, people are faced with long hours of cyber-engagement and get very little in return. High-levels of frustration and confidence-destroying interactions with apparently tragic and toxic people happen often. I often wonder what the difference is between people that enjoy and rely on social networking for hookups, dates, or finding a partner compared to those who are unsuccessful and discouraged about using them.

There are people out there that are more socially successful going out to a bar or another type of gathering where they can look someone in the eyes, flirt a little, and get what they want. For some, using chat sites or GPS-enabled applications gives the opportunity to get to know someone on a less physically direct level, but can still allow them to get to know each other through conversations about their interests and desires. Regardless of which method of interaction you choose, networking is used for connecting like-minded people together that share common interests and aspirations. It doesn't matter if it is a social party, a networking site like Facebook, or commonly considered hookup apps like Scruff.

I think the answer to many people's concerns about using these social networking opportunities lies mostly in the way these tools are used. As with many things, there are certain ways that tools can be best utilized, as well as acknowledging that there are some out there that appear more skilled at using them than others. Regardless of what type of networking you use, hopefully you are getting something positive out of it. If you are not, stop and evaluate what could be possible reasons for why it isn't working and generate some options about how you may want to try to change up your plan. Doing the same ineffective thing over and over is an incredible waste of time.

A hammer is an amazing tool if you are building a house or fixing a fence, but could absolutely be considered detrimental if it is used to attack someone by bashing their skull in when you're pissed off at them. There are also some out there that aren't skilled at using a hammer to pound in nails straight or build something that resembles anything functional. In our society, we aren't so quick to dismiss the hammer as an effective tool just because it can be used for destructive purposes or we aren't good at using it. Learning to effectively use technology-based tools is possible as well.

You can only have so many conversations using our amazing technology with the combinations of the following phrases: Hey man. What's up? Grrr. Yo! Sup? Woof. Horny? I'm not convinced that it is the fault of these social networking sites that make these exchanges so frustrating or unfulfilling. Look at the way that many individuals are using them.

It is the fault of the end-users that take these opportunities to connect with some amazing people and squander these by misusing these tools. It is ridiculous to think that it would ever be acceptable to have these types of conversations in person, so don't settle for it in cyberspace.

Rude online & nice in person

Dear Brent,

I made a profile on a hookup website and posted a few pictures of me. There was one very hot guy that I emailed, but he replied that I "wasn't in his league" and I should have read his profile closer because he has "high standards." He blocked me before I could even reply to him. Recently, I saw him at a gay bar. He's not nearly as hot as his picture, but he came over to introduce himself. After a couple minutes, he gave me his name and number, wanting to hang out sometime. I'm 100 percent sure it is the same guy but he didn't recognize me. He seems nice in person and I find him physically attractive, but I still can't get over how badly he treated me online. Should I take him out or tell him that he doesn't meet my "high standards?"

Telling him that he doesn't meet your high standards would be completely appropriate, quite funny, and so ironic. Of course there are many other ways to look at this situation. Some of them are less grumpy and energy-intensive than others, but at the end of the day it is up to each of us as individuals to figure out how to deal with challenging situations. You have the opportunity to blow off his comments, pretend you weren't impacted, crucify him, or come up with some other creative way of dealing with this social atrocity.

First of all, being directly rude and hurtful to someone that simply tells you "hello" is in extremely bad form, completely inappropriate, and should not be tolerated. The initial greeting during any interaction could mean many things depending on your intention. These may include finding someone attractive, because you are bored and looking to have some small-talk, or are interested in finding out if you have anything in common. Some people perceive a greeting as hitting on them for sex or could be translated to mean, "I want to put a ring on it and move into your house. You are my soul mate!" Sometimes a "hello" is just simply a nice way of beginning a conversation.

For some, there is a different set of online guidelines that define appropriate behaviors and language that may not be acceptable in the real world. Common courtesy does not always happen in cyberspace. Some people can be insensitive, negative, and spiteful. Before messaging someone in an attempt to engage them, check out their profile for red flags that might tip you off that they are a little tragic. These can include an over-abundance of nasty and judgmental language, an extensive list of what they don't want, or arrogance about how much they kick ass. Although misguided, there are people that may feel these behaviors are acceptable or they are using them to protect their fragile egos that have been damaged in the past. Generally, I would suggest putting these people in the "whatevabetch" category and take them out of your field of vision.

There is also a type of person that gets off on having some sense of power when hiding behind the screen. Much like the Wizard of Oz, when the big tough image is found to be an inaccurate projection and the person doesn't have the power they claim to possess, this individual doesn't come across as being so big and bad anymore. Insecurity can come out in so many ways including developing fake self-esteem or confidence by putting others down. Beware of these people. They either need to tear others down to make themselves feel better or you will end up spending a lot of time and energy trying to patch their cracked self-image.

There may be one aspect of this situation that does make some sense. For some of us, it can be difficult to match a real-life image of someone when compared to a digital copy on a website or phone application. Some people look hotter, shorter, or less attractive then their pictures while others blatantly lie and post pictures that aren't them. There is every possibility that he really doesn't link your online image to your current interaction or remember how much of a douche he was to you online.

Don't let his adorable appearance cause you amnesia. He still hurt your feelings and is now standing in front of you wanting something. At the very least, something should be said about his behaviors and how they affected you. You don't have to be overly dramatic about this, but you may help to save someone else from his hateful explosions. This confrontation may also help him take a hard look at how he acts and can have a positive impact to help him become a more thoughtful person. He may turn out to be a really nice guy or prove that you should have trusted your instincts and told him to bugger off. There are plenty of attractive, intelligent, and engaging people out there. Sometimes you just have to sort through some douchebags to find them.

Is technology making us socially retarded?

The internet is single-handedly the most amazing tool for connecting us intellectually, culturally, and socially. For all the ways it bonds us, it also serves to drive us apart and keep us from interacting. Some feel there is not a need to go out to a public place to meet people when you can safely cruise around behind your screen. For all the opportunities that technology brings to us, many of us have become its slaves. This cruel master makes some feel that there is no longer the need to search for more creative ways of connecting with people. We have traded talking for typing, laughing for LOL, and meeting people for endless online chatter. I think a lot about how we can continue to embrace technology while keeping focus on the importance of face-to-face connections.

Somehow, reliance and comfort in the online world can lead into some very concerning behaviors. For those of us who utilize technology to communicate with each other socially and for hooking up, we truly can risk losing the desire and ability to connect effectively in the real world. It is amazing that multiple hours of online chatting generally only produce a small amount of physical interaction. Worse than that, it could keep us from physical contact all together.

I wish there was an online classification system that we could put into our profiles that would designate the type of online surfer we are. These titles could include, "seriously looking to connect," "playing games and will probably never meet up with you," or "I've been up for three days and really don't care who or what I'm doing." Many of us who are serious about meeting up seem to be in the same sandbox with those who are playing some type of strange game of keep away. That is massively frustrating.

Some people get off on being rude and hurtful, while others are directly discriminatory, dismissive, and choose to use their online presence to act like a prick. It can also be used as an arena where some people feel they can spout off any ignorant, venomous comments without fear of accountability or real retaliation against them. In a society that values freedom of speech, sometimes people abuse that and act like jackasses online. Realize not every idea or opinion is valid and there are many rude and ill-informed people around us.

There are other concerning behaviors that come out of

being online that are not as intentionally hurtful, but cause many to feel frustrated with cyberspace communication. Some people online lie about many things including body type, age, and personal intentions. It could be done out of fear of rejection, not knowing what they really want, or getting off on playing games with someone. You do not always know the type of person on the other end of the conversation when you begin chatting. Some people get stuck in fantasy and show low motivation to get into the real world. Rejection and conflict may feel more hurtful when we are not hiding behind a computer screen, but that fear also keeps us from connecting with others. When you get into a disagreement with someone in a restaurant, you can't block them, report them to the webmaster, or send them straight to voicemail.

Consider your ratio of time spent online compared to meeting guys face-to-face. If you are spending significantly more time in front of your computer, maybe it is time to change some tactics. There is nothing wrong with moving an online chat to a phone conversation. This is a great way to determine if a conversation can happen organically. You also get a better impression if someone is going to be a good potential match for an in-person meeting. You can tell if they seem disinterested, dominates conversations, or can't maintain focus while they are talking to you. After good phone conversation, you could actually meet in person to do something. It doesn't have to cost a lot of money or have a huge time commitment. Meet for coffee, a walk around a park, an art show opening, or go get naked. See if any type of real connection can be made instead of living in cyberspace.

It is concerning that our fear of potential discomfort and rejection is keeping people from meeting each other. Unfortunately some people online are not focused on making these types of new connections. Social networking and online chat sites have been developed as a method to help people connect, not as a substitute for real human interaction. The only promise that an online presence affords you is a potentially increased chance of meeting someone awesome. Don't get stuck using a tool without remembering why you are using it and what you can build when used correctly.

Online socializing with intent of meeting

Dear Brent,

I am concerned about where the gay scene is headed on the issue of online socializing. I used to love it, but I'm worried now that it has become the new norm and a preferred way of getting to know people. It seems like we are all so disconnected and have lost the ability to unite on any organic level. I also fear for bars, night clubs, and other gay establishments because people aren't going out as much. Is human contact going to be reduced to one hour of combined total time chatting online, 15 minutes of sex, and then back to solitude?

Many of us remember times were we went out in public to determine if someone had an athletic build, was a great conversationalist, or kissed like Casanova. Not only am I in total agreement with your fears, but I am also a huge proponent of getting away from technology and enjoying the company of real people face-to-face. I know you're not the only one concerned about the huge amount of time people can spend online to hopefully make some kind of interpersonal or sexual connection.

Most of us are painfully aware that the time spent chatting online is generally not met with the same return on investment as we put in and it can be frustrating in many ways. There are people who boldly lie where many others have lied before. There are also those awful, miserable people that feel that acting like a jackass is a good option and they want to inflict their crappy attitude on others. Crappy online attitudes and actions can be extremely demotivating, frustrating, and hurtful to us.

We have to be careful about putting blind faith in online exchanges as a realistic expression of people's attractions and intentions. In many cases, it is easy to have some sexy talk over the internet or phone. Entire relationships and sexual scripts can be planned out before meeting in person. Many times when people do meet after an extended time of tech-based courting, it goes poorly since fantasy can sometimes be quite different than reality. Often these online passions let us down and we feel they should have remained living on the phone or in our computers. Not only can people put out an inauthentic persona, but there are just some attractions that can only be truly gauged in person. We waste time theorizing how amazing the connection will be instead of simply getting together to see what unfolds. The fantasy we create in our minds rarely is an accurate impression of real life. It's not necessarily that either person was dishonest, but many times it takes a true physical interaction to see how these dynamics actually play out.

There are so many positive life lessons that can be gained by being social with others. We can learn to confront our insecurities, challenge shyness, develop strong support networks, and discover commonalities between ourselves and others. Additionally, we can also learn to deal with rejection and may build better confidence by getting offline. Although there are aspects of security from hiding behind our technology, we can benefit ourselves more by trying to improve on these skills and challenge ourselves to be more successful and confident simply by getting physically in front of people.

Although it seems like there are many socially-deficient people out there, I'm also concerned that there are so many potential relationships with others that are missed because we are living predominantly online. Messages are misinterpreted, ignored, or get lost in the shuffle. Being online seems to come with its own set of unfortunately acceptable rules and common behaviors that are improper or ineffective in person. On the flipside, there are social skills that can be best developed and practiced within physical proximity of other people.

All of this being said, when you make an amazing linkage to another person due to a technology-facilitated method, some of the frustration and wasted times seems like less of a bummer. Don't spend precious energy and focus on those negative people and situations. There are so many more you could potentially enjoy. As much as our culture may be moving towards cyber communication and connection, it is up to us to break out of those patterns.

We don't have to be slaves to technology.

Moving from online to the real world

Dear Brent,

I feel that I'm spending a lot of unproductive time online. It seems like a huge time waster and I'm definitely not getting out of it what I'm putting into it. I'm always surprised about the high number of people that aren't really interested in meeting in person. Is it too much to ask that people actually want to do something other than send messages back and forth? Why don't people want to use these sites to go out to do other things?

In a perfect world, we are going online to increase our chances to meet quality people that could become important parts of our lives. The reality is that most of us get online because we are lonely, bored, or horny. Possibly all three all at once. One aspect of the online culture that has always confused me is the phobia that many people have of moving from the online realm into the real world. Even more confusing is how people that really want to meet in person are most often chatting with people that seem to not want to get off their computers.

When we meet new people, many of us fear that conversations will be uncomfortable or boring, there might not be a spark when you look into their eyes, or maybe neither of you will be as charismatic or funny as you are online. Chatting with someone online provides many aspects of safety. Sometimes having that extra time buffer to allow yourself to come up a witty response is much easier than being extemporaneous in person. Some people are more comfortable with online messages because they haven't developed the ability to communicate effectively with others or challenged their debilitating insecurities to enjoy meeting people.

I usually think about the statement, "they can type, but can they talk?" What is most concerning to me is that some people have gotten so stuck in the online world that they have difficulties identifying the real world as a happy place where they want to spend time. For some, being rejected online isn't as emotionally destructive as it could be at a club, but it can definitely happen more often in a shorter amount of time. The cumulative effects of negativity online can be extremely hurtful. Just because it's not face-to-face, experiencing disinterest or a nasty message from someone can be extremely cutting.

If you're online and really serious about meeting someone for offline fun, I would suggest putting this desire out there immediately and very directly. There is nothing wrong with stating that you are using a website as a tool to meet people for activities and good times, not to exchange three months of cute messages about what funny videos they found on the internet or what they want to do to you in a sexual fantasy. When conversations go like this, it can signal that the other person wants to stay in a cyber fantasy world so they don't have to deal with real human contact with you. Those people may string you along without the intention of meeting up and will continue to play avoidance games. If you want something to happen, then pursue it with someone who will actually want to hang out with you. Be wary of those people that will not show their face, talk on the phone, or meet you for a social interaction. It should make you wonder why or what are they hiding.

Taking calculated risks can allow you to move into actually hanging out with someone instead of wasting time wondering if you will hit it off. If an online chat is going well, you can move to a phone conversation. I'm not talking about 50 text messages exchanged while you're at work, but a real conversation with spoken words. After that, you could meet for a walk, quick bite or a drink. Although you may devote some time, energy, or money into hanging out with someone, it's worth it. You may not be able to use LOL, ROFL, or :-) when you are talking in person, but please feel free to wink, smile, laugh, or hug. Those were our options before the widespread use of the internet. Change your tactics with how you use these tools. Online profiles are wonderful ways of connecting with people, but quit letting them run or ruin your social life.

How to take back our social lives from technology.

There are so many of us that get extremely frustrated with our culture's reliance on the internet and other electronic formats to enhance our social lives. For all the negative and unsatisfying aspects of trying to connect in these ways, when you click with someone in person that you met online, all the time and effort can seem worth it. I want to bring up some ways to protect your head, heart, and self-esteem when pursuing these activities instead of having them make you feel crappy. These ideas are also good to keep in mind to avoid your development into one of those guys that makes other people feel injured online.

Be careful not to fall into looking for only the "perfect" option for an encounter. There are many fantastic "average" looking or sounding prospects out there that will provide you hours of enjoyment. Many people search for the absolute best possibility that you think will give them the most mind-blowing experience ever. Unfortunately most of the time when this thought process is used, it just gains more alone time staring at the computer screen. Just like you can be really funny without being a comedian, some people can be brilliant without a master's degree or screw really well without being built like a porn star. Also keep in mind that almost none of us are in the top one percent of sexy people on the planet, so quit looking for that top one percent to hit on and then be disappointed and bitter because they aren't interested in you.

Sometimes the potential awkwardness of meeting someone in person keeps us from moving past online chatting. If you are socially uncomfortable or have difficulty carrying on a conversation when you meet someone in person, work on your communication skills and quit running away from the discomfort. You learn to improve skills by practicing, not avoidance.

There are many concerning behaviors that appear to be all too common during online interactions. These include a lack of common courtesy, kindness, and honesty. Sometimes being online gives some people the feeling that being rude is OK and trying to make someone feel badly is acceptable. If someone sends you a message and you are not interested, simply respond with a "no thank you" type of response or choose not to respond. You don't have to email a scathing response intended to hurt their feelings. Don't waste energy on writing a novel about how they are not your type or how tragic you think they are.

If you are sending someone a message and they respond with any of the previously mentioned options, just suck it up and move on. Hopefully your self-esteem has not been completely destroyed and you don't retreat into your safe cave like a wounded animal. Arguing or being rude with them will not make them want to meet you or hook up anyway. If your ego is feeling fragile, try finding some other activities that make you feel more fulfilled and then go back to online surfing in limited doses until you quit feeling hurt.

I truly feel that if an online chat is going well, talk to the person on the phone or make plans to meet up and do something. There are many people that can come up with witty comments online, but can't do it spontaneously in person. Unfortunately with a lack of physical contact and social exchange, some people appear to lose the skills important in picking up on social cues like body language. It takes practice and an active interest in reading people to get good at it. There are books and classes out there that can help with building some of these skills if you're really interested in learning new techniques.

Be wary of those people who will not talk to you on the phone or are avoidant of meeting in person. Not only is there a much lower chance of ever meeting them, it may also be very possible that they are misrepresenting themselves in pretty significant ways. Some are married to women, already partnered in a "monogamous" relationship, or lying about other things. Some people are playing an online sexy persona game where they get to play the dirty vixen for a little while and get some dirty talk out of their system. Don't waste your time.

Don't forget that technology has been created to improve our quality of life, not make it more complicated or painful. Also remember that although you are looking at an electronic version of someone's profile or pictures, there is a real person represented there. Be careful not to lose your humanity or ability to connect with people face-to-face. We are all human and deserve respect, friendship, and love. Hopefully you can find balance between this incredible technology and real social interaction.

CHAPTER 3: EMOTIONS

Why do some appear stronger than others?

Dear Brent,

I have never felt comfortable dealing with stressful things that happen to me. Growing up I had numerous challenges with my family and my own self-confidence, but there are many people that I know that had it much worse than me and seem to deal with anything that comes their way. Is there a reason why some people are able to deal with life challenges and difficulties better than others?

I've always found it interesting that some people from really rough childhoods or other difficult life experiences appear to have the capacity to leave behind the hurt caused by what many of us would consider debilitating situations to become powerful, fulfilled and happy individuals. These people seemingly overcome challenges such as poverty, discrimination, abuse and other traumatic situations.

There are others that seem to develop feelings of powerlessness and can fall into patterns of feeling little control over coping with many of life's tough situations. They may perceive the world as an unfair place full of treacherous pitfalls and villains waiting to jump into their lives to disrupt it and hurt them.

A complex mix of personality characteristics, supportive situations and a healthy dose of good fortune may have the most potential positive influence in a person's ability to overcome a variety of difficulties that may arise throughout our lives without becoming a victim to their destructive forces. There is an ongoing debate about what makes some people more resilient against these difficulties than others. In our community, so many of us have struggled with feelings of inferiority, abuse, abandonment, body image, shame and other insecurities. Although most of us experience these, some appear better equipped to deal with them.

There are some personality characteristics that are thought to help people cope with difficult situations and increase the possibility that they will not fall prey to the horrors of life's unpredictable moments. Traits like having a good sense of humor, effective communication, independence and creative problem-solving skills can allow someone to feel that they can create outcomes that get them what they want without having their feelings catastrophically hurt. Resourcefulness, compassion, and the desire to take the initiative in accomplishing goals can help support a sense of self-confidence. Some are skilled in creating supportive networks of people that can aid in gaining outside perspectives while nurturing our need to connect with other good people.

Some of these strengths may appear to be innate with someone, but most times they were gained with the support from outside sources like family or friends. They can also be developed throughout our lives by gaining experience and getting through difficulties. Over time, we can gain increased awareness about some unknown strengths and abilities that were waiting inside us to be released. Tapping into these may take time, focused attention, and a lot of practice. Regardless of where they come from, they can help give us the strength and confidence to take on a variety of situations and come out of them successfully. Our ability to cope with life stresses gives us a better chance of not losing our minds when things get rough.

Although having these strengths doesn't stop crappy things from coming into our lives, they can benefit us in becoming more self-sufficient and empowered to deal with unexpected or unfortunate challenges. We have the opportunity to engage these difficult experiences with confidence to take these on with increased abilities to emerge victorious.

Finding your power

Dear Brent,

I feel that there are so many situations and people in my life that are keeping me down. I really try to not surround myself with negative or mean people, but they seem to find me and screw up my life. I'm tired of feeling that I don't have the ability to improve my life because of all these bad things happening to me and I have no control of when or how they affect me. What can I do to make myself stronger in these situations?

It sounds like you think that the universe keeps dealing you a shitty hand when it comes to people in your life, as well as things that happen to you and around you. There are many of us that struggle with feeling that our lives are not fully within our control. Although this is a totally correct impression since we are never 100 percent able to shape the world around us or how interactions and situations play out, there are often times where we allow ourselves to feel powerless to change situations even when we actually can.

This inability can cause us to feel unhappiness, frustration and grief, which keeps us down emotionally and from taking charge to improve our lives. In reality, I think we have more power than we often feel to influence the world around us. Of course, snapping your fingers and clicking your heels together won't produce a hot group of rugby players for an afternoon play session, but we can have a positive impact on our own life situations and who enriches our lives.

Think about how you may have more influence over your life than you feel right now. Take a second and use your imagination to picture your source of personal power being in the core of your chest like Iron Man. Not only does this allow us to have the energy to get off our asses and tackle challenges, hopes, dreams and fears, but it also enables us to feel that we have the ability to take control of our lives to make it better and more fulfilled.

Each of us has an internal light that encompasses all that we are. Inside us are our beliefs, passions, insecurities, dreams, pain, and aspirations. These qualities compose who we are, what gets us off, how we handle situations, and how we create our present and future. Unfortunately there are situations and people that appear to have the power to stop us from being the individual we aspire to be and living the life we desire.

Identify where you give away your power and figure out how to take it back. Although there are situations where we cannot regulate what others do, we can control our actions, thoughts, and how we react. Instead of maintaining the idea that we are just innocent bystanders getting slapped down by things out of our control, we can use our mental and emotional energy to look at how we may have assisted in creating the situation in the first place, get through these rough spots, or put safeguards in place to reduce the risk of these types of situations happening again.

If you allow yourself to believe that life is a cruel mistress that consistently makes you her bitch, then you risk feeling like a huge powerless victim of circumstances. These destructive thoughts infiltrate our minds and burrow down deep, causing us to believe that many things are beyond our control and we just need to sit there and take it. Fight back to regain control over your own personal power. Take the time to figure out what we have influence over directly and what we have control to walk away from quickly before it affects us further.

Emotional self-defense for beginners

Dear Brent,

There are so many times where I don't feel equipped to deal with the amount of emotionally hurtful people and situations in my life. When I am faced with these types of things, I just want run away and isolate in my apartment. I've never been good at dealing with conflict and it seems like it is getting worse as I get older. How can I become better at not getting stressed or hurt?

The world can absolutely feel like a warzone at times filled with enemies, pitfalls, and challenges to overcome. We can lessen the potential to feel hurt in many ways, but first we have to determine what our most common adversaries are so we can develop the best protection. These may include people, situations, or ourselves. We can find ways to strengthen the sensitive parts of us by building a protective wall that may provide defense for our emotional castle, but it could also keep us from experiencing the beauty of the surrounding realm. We could also focus on exiling the attackers out of our kingdom or find ways to push their armies back so they can't hurt us.

The best way to keep ourselves safe from hurtful situations is to not become involved with them in the first place. Surrounding ourselves with positive, supportive people and situations is ultimately important and the best defense against negativity. Most times, this provides us with low drama, more happiness, and hopefully a higher degree of personal satisfaction. Be confident that you can make healthy connections and conscious of what and who you allow into your life.

Of course there are situations and people that we do not have the ability to push completely out of our lives. It is important to develop skills that are effective in protecting our hearts since retreating isn't always an option. This may come in the forms of developing the self-confidence or assertiveness to stand up for ourselves when we feel attacked. Challenge past personal beliefs that we are powerless and don't deserve positive things in our life. Building defenses aids us in developing the confidence to tell negative people to get out of our faces or identify how our feelings may have a negative impact on how we perceive difficult situations.

Take the time to develop effective weapons instead of building up fake confidence through the creation of emotional barriers. Don't create the equivalent of a cardboard suit of armor and sword while expecting it to be effective in fighting off aggressive armies. Building up your outward appearance, taking on an arrogant personality, or acting like a bitchy queen may seem to be an effective way of keeping people from being able to hurt you on the surface, but it also serves to isolate you further from others and will not actually help you develop the skills to stand up for yourself and be assertive. It can also crack or break apart under pressure, leaving you ill-equipped to protect yourself.

There are times where our best protective shield is not large or strong enough to fight off these attacks. Know when to attack and when to retreat so you can fight again another day. There are the times where we feel that we get our asses handed to us and have to retreat to take care of our wounds. Don't shy away from engaging in these types of occurrences due to a fear of discomfort or getting hurt. It is more important to spend the time and energy working to figure out how to create the best way to strengthen our arsenal so we can keep on fighting. Get ready to figure out your defensive strategies to protect vital organs from the army of self-esteem attacking ogres. Now suit up and fight!

How traumatic experiences can impact us

Dear Brent,

Growing up gay was really hard for me and my home life was full of anger and emotional abuse. I've seen counselors occasionally throughout my life, but never really felt better. I think these bad experiences continue to have a negative impact on my current relationships and I have a hard time dealing with arguments or situations when they become aggressive or I am forced to trust other people. So many other parts of my life are great, so why do these experiences continue to impact me?

What you are describing is something that happens to many people experiencing traumatic situations. It can impact us in a variety of ways, regardless if it happened to us when we were seven years old or last week. Emotional, physical, or sexual abuse or those types of situations that have a significant negative impact on us can permeate so many aspects of our relationships, both with other people and internally with ourselves. The past may influence how we deal with situations which involve anger, confrontation, reliance on other people or a number of other challenges in our lives. These experiences can also diminish our confidence, conviction, and self-esteem while causing isolation and hopelessness. In extreme cases, these experiences can lead into a desire to stop the pain by committing suicide.

There are many situations that can be classified as traumatic, not only those caused by abuse. Being gay for most of us has been extremely difficult at various times in our lives and may continue to cause negativity currently. Other conditions such as social anxiety or awkwardness, poor body image, cheating, homelessness, financial stress, arguments, or dramatic relationships can also cause us to experience very strong aftershocks. Some people fail to recognize how these types of situations impacted them when they originally happened, but also how they unfortunately continue to affect their current lives.

Healing from trauma can be addressed in a variety of ways, but it generally involves taking the time and energy to analyze these situations and how they affected you when they happened as well as how they continue to influence parts of your life. It can be hard to accept that these situations were out of your control when they happened or feel that you should have made different choices in the past. Some also become angry because they are still feeling affected by them and don't know how to release those feelings.

Be patient, it takes time to heal. Be careful about avoiding the important work that needs to be done. Also, be aware of the desire to rush through this process of healing. Many of us want to get through stressful, difficult or painful experiences as quickly as possible. Unfortunately this will most likely take some time. Allow yourself opportunities to experience your feelings and work toward resolving them. Pushing them down, ignoring them, or doing activities to numb yourself doesn't help you work through these and can actually cause more difficulties when you actually face them. As time goes on, it may become increasingly hard to deal with these issues when compounded by the fear of dealing with them. It causes us to experience more discomfort and can impede our progress.

Utilizing support from a good friend or a qualified counselor can be a beneficial addition to the process, but very few things will make this a painless endeavor. Difficult aspects of our lives are rarely easy to overcome. There will most likely be tears, anger, frustration, and fear when thinking about working on these issues. A desire to avoid or run away is also normal because it is going to be uncomfortable. Fight through these feelings that keep you from dealing with your past difficult situations so you can tackle them head-on. They don't need to continue causing unnecessary contention in your life.

Don't be afraid of fear

Dear Brent,

I get so freaked out in social situations. Having chats online is a little better, but I still don't know what to say to people or how to keep a conversation going. My fear of being seen as weird or rejected by someone keeps me from going out and trying to meet people. How can I get over being afraid and start having more fun?

Fear is definitely a normal part of our everyday life. We watch how fast we drive in certain areas for fear of a speeding ticket or set our alarms in the morning because we afraid of not waking up on time to go to work. There are some fears that serve to keep us safe from harm, but others exist to reinforce our insecurities and keep us from pursuing activities that may intrigue or interest us. These hurtful ones make our heads spin or cause a huge emotional freak out. Social interactions can be extremely challenging for many people by bringing up our own feelings of inadequacy, discomfort, and awkwardness.

Don't let fear keep you from going after something you want. Much like that monster that lived under our beds or in our closets growing up, fear exists in the darkness and is generally a figment of our imagination. We need to turn on the lights and realize that these fears that are keeping us from forming relationships and are really just our own insecurities coming out. Developing the courage to face these monsters head-on may freak us out, but it is extremely important to realize that they do not have as much power to impact our lives negatively as we think they do.

I'm not suggesting you immediately attempt to conquer your fear of socializing by throwing yourself into a big gay circuit party, but there are some smaller steps that you can do to start addressing your concerns in social situations. It doesn't matter if a person is standing in front of us or typing online, similar fears exist.

Basically, we are afraid of rejection and people being mean to us.

Don't let disinterest or a non-response from someone destroy you. Realize that some people online are only there checking out pictures or to hook up with someone that matches exactly what they are looking for at that moment. If someone doesn't respond to your message or says that they aren't interested, it is not the end of the world or a reflection on your own self-worth. Some people believe rejection hurts worse in person, but it is still a refusal regardless of how you look at it. It is hard to convince someone not to take it personally, but it is something important to work on if you are going to develop the confidence to put yourself out more in hopes of connecting with people.

Don't wait for a perfect moment to approach someone or waste time on cheesy pick-up lines. Take a moment to breathe deeply and not allow your stress levels to get out of control. Regain control of your anxious thoughts and increased heart rate so you can chill out before you talk to someone. Think about how courageous you are by facing your fears. Get ready to put on your best game face and enter the situation with confidence. Work on developing skills around small talk and putting out confidence without being cocky. Just be authentic, honest, and nice. In public, be aware of your smile, body language, eye contact, and fresh breath. It is a lot of separate things to remember at once, but with practice, all of these aspects of becoming social combine into a single presentation that takes less conscious thought after it has been practiced many times.

You can proceed with caution, but don't stop trying new things. Getting knocked down is just a part of life. We get back up, learn from the situation, and try again. The worst-case scenario is that they act like a jackass to you by rolling their eyes or turning their back. Those people can piss off and you can move on to finding a great person to hang with. Through practice, these social interactions become easier to start and our techniques to keep them rolling get more refined and effective.

Why should someone be proud of being gay?

Dear Brent,

I hear the phrase, "gay pride" thrown around all the time, but I don't think that I have ever really felt it. I'm comfortable with being gay, but why would someone be proud of it? I'm not a fan of gay bars or those people that wear their sexuality on their sleeve. I've never been to a pride parade, but it seems like it is just a bunch of people getting attention on the news for being obscene in public. I'm a normal acting man that just happens to be sexually attracted to other men. Are there other people out there like me?

The short answer is yes, but I think your question goes deeper. There is a huge difference between being involved in a variety of aspects of gay life and being a screaming queen that is totally flamboyant and covered in glittered short-shorts. Your question seems to show somewhat of a distain for people that choose to become invested in the gay community for anything other than to find a mate or for sex. While some people feel that being gay is limited to bars and pride parades, I think it offers more.

The media of course loves to push sensationalized stories involving gay people. We have sex scandals involving married pastors and drugs, while others get dressed in drag and make out with each other in front of cameras during festivals. We've historically been accused of frequent pedophilia and perversion. Unfortunately this may cause concern for you and some other people to question why feeling a sense of pride about being gay is a positive move.

I do, however, understand why some feel a sense of pride about accepting who they are as a gay individual.

First of all, there are many of us that have struggled throughout our lives to understand why we are attracted to the same sex, figure out how we want to present ourselves publically and not be terrified that we will be rejected or hurt because of who we are or choose to love. Sometimes this type of personal strife can make us feel a sense of shame about the parts of us that may cause our lives to be difficult. We might even feel like rejecting those things completely or hiding them from the general world is a safer option than accepting them as part of us. If this is the case, a person may choose to not take part in "gay" activities or go to "gay" places. Other people just don't feel like they fit in to various parts of gay culture and choose to not engage with it directly or those who feel a strong kinship to it. Thankfully there is not a checklist of places and activities you need to engage in monthly to maintain your membership in the club.

Coming out publically is another issue that can be very challenging for many people and may influence their decision to feel aspects of pride about being gay. Sexuality can be considered such a strong defining trait in somebody's life, but it is also one of the few aspects of ourselves that is commonly either embraced or rejected by others. It only takes a few instances where we are treated badly because of our sexual orientation to make us feel apprehensive about these repercussions.

In our general culture, there isn't a lot of discrimination because someone defines themselves as heterosexual and usually straight people don't have to come out for being attracted to the opposite sex. Our process of working to accept our sexuality leads to many shared experiences that make us feel strange because of our attractions, especially growing up. Having unity with others that share similar struggles and journeys can make us feel less unusual. Some even feel that there is somewhat of a basic brotherhood within the community because of these experiences.

To feel like you are not part of the "gay crowd" may mean that you haven't found the right group of gay men yet. There is also a possibility that you have shaped a rigid idea of what it is like to be gay and convinced yourself that there is not a place for you that would not be stereotypical or too over the top. I would ask that you take some time and think about why you feel that.

There is a lot of diversity out there and so many things that make up our gay culture that define us as a group. Although this may include gay bars and pride parades, it is much more expansive than just that. We share some type of cultural history full of challenges and successes. Some share an interest in artistic endeavors, food, camping, or even football. There are many ways to become engaged in the "gay scene" and with other gay people.

I love the idea of gay pride and public events where queer people and straight allies can come together to show support for each other while bringing awareness to concerns about equality and acceptance. Personally I am thankful that part of gay culture includes cocktails, parties, and lots of fun. I am also grateful that it is so much more. I enjoy seeing public events where diversity and solidarity are the main themes. Watching people who care about each other and are focused on social change makes me feel supported and powerful. You don't have to parade down the street covered in rainbow paraphernalia from head to toe to show gay pride, but hopefully you can look in the mirror at yourself or stare into the eyes of a guy you really like and feel proud and happy to be part of a larger wonderful community.

So what is love anyway?

I am fascinated with the concept of love. This single word conveys such a wide variety of feelings and can mean different things to different people. It can cause a few to run in terror or be a welcomed sentiment when you feel connected to someone special. Love can be used to describe relationships with your family, friends, pets, or cuddle buddies. It can be an extremely healthy emotion and expression of dedication, while also potentially existing to cause drama in our lives. This is one of the most common words to describe something wonderful, but unfortunately is also often misused, misconstrued and abused.

When love exists, we are elated and look forward to more experiences where we can feel it. When ripped from us, we may feel a great loss and wonder when love will come around again. Some wonder if they have ever actually felt love or when that magic moment will happen to them, especially in the context of a relationship. Craving these types of feelings can drive us to actively search them out in our lives and make them a priority to find. This noble quest may lead us to feel that without love, our lives are not truly complete. This motivation can also influence us to jump from one relationship to another, looking for an individual who has the potential to fulfill us. This beautiful experience can turn ugly quite quickly if it is with the wrong individual or situation.

Take the time to think about why you are using the word love and its importance to you before it is expressed. Some people use this word to describe a concept that they may not completely understand or think sounds like a good thing to say to someone without thinking about the ramifications. It may also be expressed uncontrollably in the heat of the moment. Regardless, consider how you mean to use it and why it is coming out of your mouth. The accurate use of this word is a fantastic way to describe the emotional, physical, intellectual, social and passionate connection between people. Our relationships with others exist to help give our lives meaning by creating opportunities to explore things which make us smile and motivate us to continue creating a life we love living. Don't allow this beautiful word to become something hurtful and negative for us. Use it when our hearts really feel it.

CHAPTER 4: SKILLS DEVELOPMENT

Social discomfort

Dear Brent,

I want a relationship, but I don't think I'm as comfortable socially as most people and definitely don't feel that I am as attractive as a lot of other guys. I don't have much experience going to bars or clubs and feel that I won't be able to meet anyone there anyway. Do you have ideas on how I can improve my social skills so I won't feel awkward among all of these intimidating guys? I really want to meet someone to date.

We are all searching for something regardless if it is a better job, more time for hobbies, bigger muscles, or that special relationship with someone. One thing that ties all of these aspirations together is that our success is based on our ability to remain focused on that goal while we work to achieve it. To accomplish anything in our life, we have to figure out what we want and develop a plan on how to get it. We also need to determine which tools are important to develop and what sacrifices are we willing to make to get what we want.

There is a small part of our population that has natural tendencies for being socially dynamic, charismatic, and ultimately popular. Sometimes these people may peak early and have a quick decline as they get older. Many queer people have awkward beginnings as we struggle with self-acceptance and expressions of our sexuality, but can grow more socially comfortable later in life as we become more comfortable with ourselves and find people that appreciate and enjoy our company.

Many people look at the accomplishments or qualities of others and feel that they want it, but don't have any idea of how to get it. It is difficult to know what these people actually have or what they have achieved. At times we see others through our own set of experiences and assumptions, but these impressions can be notoriously wrong since they are only based on our surface impressions. We may also be experiencing jealousy, anger, or frustration that we are not happy or haven't achieved something that we truly feel we want. It's easier at times to become judgmental of other people than to look internally about how we feel about our own accomplishments and challenges.

Unfortunately, these perceptions may lead us into making judgments about other people. Sometimes this can be used to psych ourselves out so we don't approach people. We convince ourselves that we will be turned down by someone before we even talk to them. We convince ourselves that we are not worthy, interesting, or attractive enough to talk to someone who intimidates us or that they are probably not looking for someone like us because of some imagined list of requirements that we cannot provide to them.

Our lack of healthy self-esteem can be one of the most detrimental qualities that keeps us from pursuing conversations or potential relationships. There are an infinite number of reasons why our self-esteem can be in the toilet, but takes a strong personal initiative to overcome it. We have to actively challenge those ideas over and over to convince ourselves that they are not accurate and have little use for us to continue believing. Those repetitive beliefs may be at the core of what is limiting you socially and should be addressed.

When we get stuck in comparing ourselves with others or are in a crappy mindset, we risk limiting our actions depending on how we are feeling at that moment. If we are feeling good about ourselves, we may take a chance and approach someone we find hot or intriguing, but if we are slaves to feeling inadequate, we are going to stand on the sidelines feeling awkward, undesirable, and rejected. Challenging ideas that you are not as dynamic or eye-catching as other people sets you up for failure before you even have a chance to be successful.

Unfortunately, most of us do not take opportunities to approach someone that intimidates us to find out who they really are and what qualities they have. In reality, no one really should ever make us feel that we are not worthy individuals. You don't know what hardships, challenges, or struggles someone has gone through in their lives by simply looking at them. There are many financially successful people that have failed in business ventures and some incredibly buff people that were fat kids. Be very careful about assuming anything, especially because most of us hate it when people assume things about us.

There are many skills that can benefit us in becoming more comfortable socially. Working on overcoming low self-esteem is one of the most powerful improvements we can make. Change can take time and a significant amount of effort. Nothing needs to come easily, so don't expect it. Over time, these personal improvements become more natural and require less active thought. Don't give up on the idea that change is possible and you can achieve what you want.

Clueless about social cues

Dear Brent,

I have a hard time reading if someone is checking me out or wants to come up to talk. I'm also really bad about knowing if I'm annoying someone or if they are even interested in talking to me. It feels like there are times when I feel like I'm in a foreign environment where I don't know or understand the culture or social rules. What would you suggest doing to become more aware about how others feel?

One of the most complicated skills to develop is how to become aware of social cues and use them correctly. You have to put out your own intentions to people, interpret the interests of others, decide if you want to engage that person, and then figure out the most effective way to interact with them to hopefully get what you want. You can spend a lifetime and read lots of literature, acquiring suggestions about how to read body language, flirt, have small talk, and hopefully make a great connection with someone. Here are a few of the most helpful ones that have worked for me.

The first step is to figure out if there is a potential interest from the object of your affection. Check out how they make or maintain eye contact with you. A simple smile and good eye contact can signal interest on your part, but they may also give you a quick head nod and a grin. This can show that your message has been received and accepted, but they also may not have noticed you sent this signal or think it was just a passing glance. Maybe you were just throwing out a general greeting and you aren't necessarily interested in talking to them. There are many variables to consider and possible outcomes that can happen. You may have to engage them to know how they feel about talking to you. Many times this is the most difficult situation to navigate because it challenges us to face our fears of potential rejection. It truly is the best way to find out if someone is potentially interested in us, even if it is just for a brief chat that could lead into something else.

My next suggestion would be to ditch your "end goal" and just enjoy the moment of interacting and hanging out with someone. If you are singularly focused on getting laid or gaining a great partner, there is an increased possibility that you will come across as desperate, awkward or pushy. It also may stop you from picking up on accurate messages from the other person. You might want to completely bowl over anything that your unsuspecting target wants since you are going to try to achieve your goal at any cost. Not only does it provide an uncomfortable interactive situation for two people, but you probably risk feeling like a failure if you can't seal the deal. Change your perspective about having to gain something specific out of talking to someone. Use these situations as opportunities to practice small talk and enjoy getting to know people. Through these interactions you can be introduced to new and exciting people, places, and activities.

I think one of the main problems with trying to figure out social cues is that our own insecurities tend to taint our perceptions. It may convince us that we are too weird or definitely not what the other person is looking for. Remember we are not psychic and don't necessarily know what the other person is thinking. Don't use this as an excuse for not practicing your social skills and approaching someone to start a dialogue.

My last suggestion is to open your eyes and take some time to observe others around you. Think of this as somewhat of a sociological experiment where we learn by watching people. There is not a magic formula that creates successful social people, but you can watch the body language, approaching methods, and physical contact style of people that appear to engage others in ways that you want to try. Then you can attempt some things during your own interactions that you think have the potential to be effective for you. There is nothing wrong with using techniques that have already been proven effective by others. Don't be scared to experiment with a variety of approaches and you can even combine a variety of techniques. Find the ones that give you the best outcomes. Keep in mind that these skills take practice and will get better over time.

Socially unapproachable

Dear Brent,

When I go out by myself, I am usually stuck standing against the wall and people don't talk to me. I have been told that I look mean and unapproachable, but I'm a really nice guy. I'm extremely shy and I don't know how to connect with people socially. Unfortunately other people aren't coming up to me either. I don't feel confident enough to try different methods of meeting people, but I know that it is important to change how I come across. How do I overcome some of my old patterns so I can meet people while I'm out?

One of the biggest problems with this is when you feel uncomfortable, your body language may be your worst enemy. Going out with a buddy or a group can provide some buffers against feeling lonely or socially awkward. At times it takes a lot of courage to go out on your own.

Non-verbal communication has the ability to communicate things to people before you even get a chance to ask how their night is going or compliment them on their adorable outfit. Your body posture, eye movements, and facial expressions can set you up for potential success or give the impression that you would rather be at home clipping your toenails. Although you want someone to get to know you for your strengths, interests, and passions, your outward appearance will most likely be the first set of qualities others will see and their interest in that can lead into your first conversation.

Take a hard look about how you are feeling about yourself before you walk into a social place. Realize that if you are getting stressed out about going out, feeling bloated, or are having an "all gay men suck" moment, you are most likely going to be outwardly expressing some of these internal feelings that are not going to motivate others to approach you. There may be times where you are going to have to consciously act differently on the outside than you feel on the inside. Although your anxiety levels may be through the roof or you don't feel comfortable in a particular environment, you do not have to put that out in your body language. Over time, telling yourself that you are mellow, confident, and enjoy the opportunity to be around other people may allow your mind to begin believing those feelings and can actually calm down anxious feelings. Going in with a positive attitude is going to be your most powerful ally in the fight to be more socially approachable.

Be aware of how you may be appearing to other people. They may be checking out the way you are standing, if you look uncomfortable, or if you just scratched your ass or sniffed your armpit. Not to make you paranoid, but someone always may be looking at you as you stand awkwardly against the wall. Be careful about how much time you spend checking your phone, picking your fingernails, or fidgeting with your shirt. Some people rock back and forth, tap their foot, or play air drums when they are feeling out of place. Those people may also have their shoulders rounded, hands in their pockets, head down, shuffling their feet, or be frowning. Think about how you would define someone's body language that is confident. They are standing tall with their shoulders back and chest out. They are ready for it to be showtime!

Maintaining eye contact with someone you want to talk to is very important. It can show interest in them, but also confidence in yourself by not looking away and down at your shoes immediately after locking eyes with them. Be careful not to look like a crazy stalker or try to stare them down. If eye contact is made, a little smile is great or a head nod is totally fine. Sticking your tongue out to simulate licking parts of their body may be considered over the top. A reciprocating grin, head nod, or smile can signal that there is some interest, so get your ass over there and begin a chat. Having confidence to move from non-verbal interaction to a full-on verbal exchange shows that you are working to become more successful than you have been in the past. It causes us to face our own insecurities by allowing us to experience what it feels like to complete tasks like these. They can become much easier over time depending on how many times we practice them.

A great tool to discover what your body language may possibly be saying to others is to gain impressions from your friends, but only if they are going to give you honest feedback. Don't ask those people who will just say, "yes darling, you are absolutely fantastic." Although some feedback can be difficult to hear, remember that it can help you improve your ability to be more approachable. At the end of the day, you have to decide what will work for you, but getting other's impressions can be helpful. Keep in mind that this is not a comprehensive system on how to attract people with your body language, just some ideas and suggestions. Next time you want to go out socially, try something new and continue experimenting.

Getting in the mood to be social

Dear Brent,

I know that my social skills are not at the level I want them to be and I feel uncomfortable when I try connecting with people. I've been reading your column for a long time and you are always pushing people to meet up in person to develop friendships and relationships, but I don't feel that I have the confidence to even begin trying to do this in person. What suggestions do you have to get me started?

I grew up as an extremely awkward, introverted kid with questionable self-esteem. Unfortunately it carried into most of my early adulthood as well. Throughout the years, I was extremely jealous of those people that seemed to navigate social encounters, be surrounded by great friends, and were able to just exist in their environment without looking uncomfortable. Eventually I learned that not only was I not alone in these feelings, but I had the ability to work on gaining these skills. Attaining them was ultimately important if I wanted to gain the confidence to connect with people and feel better about my life.

There are so many perspectives about how to do this. In my experiences, the mindset you maintain when approaching difficult or uncomfortable situations is one of the most important aspects in determining success and motivating you to keep trying to improve. Here are some suggestions designed to get your head in a good place before your mouth opens. Hopefully, this helps you develop more internal strength, confidence, and an increased positive outlook in your efforts to become more socially comfortable and engaged.

A good technique to try when feeling higher levels of stress or anxiety when socializing is just simply to breathe. Without oxygen, your body doesn't function correctly and this stress can cause an increased cycle of internal freakout. Take in a few really deep breaths. With every full exhale, envision that the feelings of being a socially-awkward dude are leaving your body. With every inhale, replace those insecure thoughts and perceptions with the energy of feeling confident about who you are, what interests you, and that you're a great person. Not only will this help to start replacing negative thoughts and feelings with healthier ones, but also to slow your body and mind down so you can more effectively deal with the fact that you are freaking out. You can do this in the car, outside of a building, in a bathroom stall, or covertly within a group of people. Slowing down your breathing, heart rate, and racing thoughts can remove some of the uncomfortable feelings of anxiety and discomfort. It's more of a technique to calm yourself down in any high-stress situation, not just when you are getting into something social.

Your mindset often has an impact on your expression of personal body language, including how you stand, look at others and clinch your jaw. It is important to be conscious of how you may appear to other people. Looking under-confident, standoffish or arrogant can act as a barrier to people wanting to approach and talk to you. Many times, these types of looks come from feeling insecure inside and put out non-verbal cues to others around you. Unfortunately, this can cause social failure before anyone has the opportunity to get to know you. This can reinforce your feelings of being socially undesirable and unsuccessful since people are probably staying away from you.

Another technique to keep in mind when getting in the right mindset to socialize is to remember that we all have our insecurities. Yes, even the really hot and successful guys have them. In reality, many people are significantly insecure about something within themselves, however some are much better at covering it up. It is extremely important to take the time and energy to address these issues, but that can happen over time. You can use this knowledge to your advantage by reminding yourself that in many ways we all struggle with personal identity, body image, success, happiness and fulfillment.

You are not alone and chances are that the person you want to hang out with experiences similar challenges as well.

A positive mindset will benefit you more than any cheesy pickup line or gimmick. There are almost no guarantees about anything in this world, but getting your mind, heart, and body in alignment before challenging yourself to be social is a great idea. This is just one aspect of the importance of developing a strong list of tips and tricks that help people become more successful when trying to engage socially. Keep in mind that before any of these skills are truly effective, you have to also work on taking care of the awkward kid inside of us. He can heal from all the past difficulties and grow into a more confident man that enjoys the company of other strong people.

Starting conversations

Dear Brent,

I really just don't know how to start talking to someone when I am at a bar or party. If I'm with friends it is easy to just hang out. But if I am somewhere alone all I do is stay out of the mix and try not to look awkward. What suggestions do you have so I can meet people by talking with them?

If you don't feel confident in your ability to go out and be a successful social stud, don't worry. These series of skills can be learned, but it takes time and practice to perfect them. It can be challenging to build the confidence to approach people, but it is more important to have something interesting to say when you engage them. Initial conversations can start with a nice simple greeting and move on to some other type of small talk. Hopefully it will move to a chat about each other's lives and interests.

When you're getting to know someone, think about how you are presenting yourself. Keep in mind not to tell your life story, everything traumatic that has ever happened to you, or all the things you are working on in therapy during your first conversation. This introduction should establish a foundation to build on. I think one of the most important things to keep in mind when getting to know someone initially is that being authentic and honest is always a good philosophy. Being nice and sweet is also extremely important. Truthful communication could also include the fact that you are not terribly comfortable going up to someone you don't know, but you are trying to meet new people and break out of your shell more. You can admit that this is a new endeavor for you, but you're trying to live more in the moment and work on new skills. That type of honesty can be quite charming.

Compliments can be a really nice way to begin a conversation with someone new, but they should be realistic and appropriately given. Telling someone you like their shirt, suit, jeans, chaps, shoes, tattoo, piercings, eyes, teeth, ears, chest, calves, butt, haircut, laugh, smile, walk, or dancing style is a completely acceptable way to begin a conversation with someone. Don't spend the majority of this interaction "hero worshipping" a well-developed body part on them or expressing how ridiculously good looking they are. Also telling him that he is the hottest man you have ever seen is not only untrue and unrealistic, but it can come across as a creepy and dishonest way to try to get into his pants.

You can also try some small talk. Relying on discussing some basic items like the weather, recent musical performances at the Grammy's, or an upcoming art opening can be a great place to start. This is where some planning can be helpful so you don't stumble over your words or ideas. If you're at the gym you can ask for someone to spot you while you are doing a bench press or you can ask a suggestion on where to buy a great new pair of sneakers.

Pick up lines are rarely successful in beginning conversations with people you don't know. If they come across as being inappropriate, stupid, dishonest, annoying, or eerie, you are definitely not going to get anywhere by using them. Trust me, telling someone that you want to be an astronaut tonight so that you can explore Uranus will most likely allow you to get a good look at his ass as he walks quickly away from you. You may also get a series of strange looks from others and develop a reputation for being extremely cheesy and weird.

You may also want to start thinking about how you would answer some basic questions that could come up frequently during these interactions. Questions about what you do for work or enjoy doing in your free time are legitimate questions to ask if someone wants to get to know you or while making small talk. It is your choice to make it as bland or exciting as you want. You can give a concise answer or make it totally long-winded. Regardless, this is your opportunity to sell yourself to someone in hopes of moving from a short conversation to a potential activity where you can get to know each other more. We have all heard the expression, "you never get a second chance to make a first impression." Make this one count.

Keep in mind that reading a book about riding a bike doesn't give you the ability to ride one. Hopefully you feel empowered and motivated to try some of these techniques to increase your effectiveness in connecting with people. Sometimes you may wreck socially and skin your emotional knee, but don't let it stop you from sucking it up and trying again. Failure is a natural part of learning anything new. Don't expect to be successful 100 percent of the time, but also don't allow fear of failure or rejection keep you from putting yourself out there. Track your successes when utilizing these techniques, work on making them seem less rehearsed, and make some mental notes on how to improve on them for future encounters.

Social skill bootcamp

I guess there are a few people that have just been graced with remarkable social skills that make them the life of the party and have afforded them amazing friends with all the wonderful fun that accompanies this success. But the truth is that most of the people that exhibit these qualities have had to overcome feelings of awkwardness or inadequacy from their past.

Most likely they were not the most popular kids and struggled with making friends and gaining acceptance from others or themselves. Something changed in their lives that has supported their development into more social creatures. Thankfully, as with many other aspects in our lives, these social activities are simply a set of skills can be taught, practiced and mastered. So much of our inability or failures when trying to socialize with others are dictated by our own insecurities. It's hard to go into a social situation with lower self-esteem or self-confidence and expect to kick ass and feel comfortable.

Learning how to be socially successful truly is more like learning how to do something athletic. It comes down to focus, training, practice and patience. Just like going to the gym to get your biceps bigger and your back stronger, your social muscles need to be developed as well. If you think that yours are really weak, these techniques and exercises can help strengthen your social skills. These are not guaranteed to get you laid more or find you that perfect partner with the white picket fence and a well-equipped dungeon downstairs, but they can help you overcome some insecurity and increase your chances of meeting some great people.

This first set of exercises happens before you utter a word to someone. After you identify a person you want to talk to, start the interaction with something simple like a smile, head nod, or a quick wave. Be careful of staring them down or looking away too quickly. You don't have to rush over right away and pounce on them like a hungry tiger hunting his next meal. Take your time and be smooth. Sometimes the person we want to talk to is in a group with others. This is not the great Persian army and you can approach them without getting attacked. You can break into the group to talk to someone without stepping on toes or interrupting a conversation. Wait for a break in the action and say hello. Don't wait for the perfect opportunity to initiate a greeting because it probably won't come. You can stand by them within their line of sight and hopefully they will engage you, but you can also wait for a lull in the conversation to begin talking to one of the members. You can move conversations around to the one you really want to engage later.

The next set of exercises occurs after you have built up the resolve to become verbal. You can just approach people and simply give a greeting before starting some small talk. You don't have to waste time or energy on cheesy pickup lines. I would also suggest having a few pieces of introductory statements in mind that you can use. You can talk about your enjoyment of the event or give an appropriate compliment. I would strongly suggest that you not discuss how much you are currently enjoying the free show of their big package. Keep your conversation and comments positive, honest, and thoughtful. Bitching about something right off the bat could show that you are a bitter person - even if you aren't - and may make them question spending further time with you. Be careful about considering these casual conversations pointless since they are generally about topics that are not crucial to discovering a cure for cancer or finding solutions to international conflict. They are great training exercises and extremely important to our social development.

Lastly, I'm about to give you one of my most treasured secrets. Talk to people like you already know them. I don't mean giving them crap like you do with a buddy, but talk to them with the confidence and comfort of talking to a friend. If you chat without making it seem like you are terribly uncomfortable, it will put them at ease, but also may help to make you relax a little. Don't have an agenda. Your primary goal is to talk to someone and get some practice in chatting with people you don't know. Your secondary goal is to see if grabbing coffee, food, or a hike could be in your future or maybe another form of sweaty encounter could happen. Also, be careful of trying to seal the deal too quickly. Take your time and try to enjoy the process without concern that you will achieve a particular outcome. It is important to develop the confidence and comfort with talking to people.

Top 10 ways to move from flirting dud to a connecting stud

Getting out and about offers us great opportunities to meet new people and have fun. Here are some ideas about how to fine tune your ability to throw out and pick up a variety of social cues that can show potential interest in pursuing a conversation or engaging in sweaty activities with others. It would be unfortunate to miss out on a chance build some great relationships with entertaining people. These are merely techniques that I have found to be extremely helpful and effective in meeting new people and developing strong and interesting friendships. If at first you don't succeed, try again or change your tactics. There is definitely no single way to be successful socially.

Remain thoughtful.

It doesn't matter if the guy is the hottest stud you have ever seen. It's not going to be effective to drool, stare him down, or maul him like a lion would attack a gazelle. On the flip-side, don't be rude or cruel to someone that you're not interested in after they hit on you or give you a compliment. If you're not interested, just say "no thank you" and move on. Being a nice guy never goes out of style.

Respect personal bubbles.

Unwelcomed invasion of someone's personal space can cause awkwardness and discomfort, but a well-executed incursion can also show interest and they may want to spend time in your bubble in return. By the way, mints are always a good option before starting the invasion.

Become emotionally aware.

Think about your attitude before you go to socialize with people. You may be feeling out of place, angry, relaxed, self-loathing, board, excited, or desperate. These can definitely come out even if you are trying hard to cover them up. It usually produces more effective outcomes to do an attitude adjustment before trying to connect with people.

Body contact is awesome.

Physical contact feels great. Don't be afraid to reach out and touch someone. Grab his arm or leg to show that you are interested, but not too hard. There is a huge difference between a gentle touch on the shoulder when laughing during a conversation and a crotch grab. Keep it appropriate until it's time to get a little more intimate.

Wear clothes that make you feel powerful and confident.

Although comfort can be important, what you wear should make you look and feel good. Feel free to ask for the feedback of some good buddies on what you're wearing. You can even take them shopping or borrow some of their gear. There is nothing wrong with a little healthy feeling of "hell yeah I look really great, now let's bring it on!"

Interpret social cues.

There is a huge difference between making eye contact and looking away because someone is shy versus looking away because they aren't attracted or want to engage in a conversation. It is important to distinguish between interest and disinterest, but sometimes you can't be sure until you go up and talk to them. Many of these things are open to interpretation. Be careful about reading too much or too little into these exchanges.

Watch your physical appearance.

The way you stand and the expression on your face tells people about you before uttering a word. Take a moment and evaluate how others may perceive you. Although your actions may not be what you are intending to put out to those around you, it may be coming across that way. If you have any doubt, take note and go stand in front of a mirror or ask a buddy for their assessment.

Look confident without overacting.

Playing games where you try to appear over-confident may give others the impression that you are arrogant, stand-offish, and unapproachable when you really want people to talk to you. Don't waste time attempting to develop an inflated ego persona. Work on feeling as comfortable as possible in social situations and breathe through uncomfortable feelings. Relax and enjoy your time out with other people.

Open your eyes.

None of these cues will be worth a damn if you don't open your eyes and recognize them. It is also extremely important to realize when they are not there. It is up to you to act appropriately in social situations regardless of how you feel internally. Be careful to not let your past experiences override your logical mind by leading you down the road of insecurity and bitterness. Many emotions have the ability to taint perceptions and may lead to making choices that don't benefit us. Also it's important to put our phones down so we can work on becoming aware of our surroundings. Many things are missed because we are looking down or away from life going on around us.

Grow a pair.

These behaviors are so much more effective when delivered by a confident person. I'm painfully aware that is can be extremely difficult to challenge feelings of insecurity to improve self-esteem. Take the time to address these and work on developing effective social skills and self-confidence. Feeling awkward and isolated can keep us from connecting with people, but more importantly from finding happiness and fulfillment in life.

Top 10 secret ways to increase your chances of connecting with someone

Hopefully we all have all been blessed with some wonderful people and fantastic opportunities in our lives. It is important to continually challenge ourselves to improve our social and supportive connections with people that are around to amuse, challenge, and love us. If this process is frustrating or difficult for you, here are some helpful techniques to assist you in improving your chances to connect with people.

Don't look desperate or super intense.

Desperation is the nasty step-sister of low self-esteem and can be detected from across a room before the first word is spoken by someone. Looking too intense can also keep someone from approaching you while staring someone down doesn't necessarily show interest. Usually it signals a creepy obsession or extremely questionable social skills. Most people run when someone brings up red flag characteristics like stalker, bitchy queen or tragic.

It's not a failure if you don't get laid.

Although this might be your primary purpose when approaching a particular someone, realize that it may not happen. It might not happen today, but maybe later. Hopefully there is something else that intrigues you about the person in case the humping doesn't happen. Take some time to find out if they are capable of doing anything else positive in your life other than to get you off.

There isn't a bad place to flirt.

Where ever you go, there are usually opportunities to work on eye contact, smiling, and small talk. The world is your training ground, so get to practicing so when it matters you will have confidence in your skills. Until you become an expert, practice will hopefully make perfect. Try this at the grocery store, movie theatre or local coffee shop. It is not always about flirting only with people you are attracted to. Work on being nice and engaging with a range of people. It is good practice for when it really counts.

You don't have to always move in for the kill.

Sometimes playing it cool is a great option. You don't have to approach people and talk to them right away. Flirting can be a great way to have a little fun history with someone before you meet. The trick is to move from the non-verbal checking out to actually meeting them eventually. Getting stuck in a long-distance exchange with no follow through is a crappy place to be as well.

Maintain eye contact.

Stop letting your discomfort lead you into looking away too soon after you have locked eyes with someone. If you immediately look away or act like you just lost your contact on the ground before running away, it shows a lack of self-confidence or potentially no interest in the other person. Maintaining eye contact for a few seconds gives you an opportunity to show that you are assertively checking them out and have the confidence to follow it up with a greeting. While you lock eyes, this is also a great opportunity to have him notice your stunning smile.

Don't use overt sexual gestures or language.

Seriously, don't think this will really turn someone on or get them to touch you. Suck your tongue back in your mouth, get your hand off your crotch, and quit pinching your nipples. Go talk to him. When you do, don't start with how much you want to lick their tattoo or squeeze their perfect butt. Keep your hands off their delicate parts until it appears to be a mutually beneficial groping opportunity for all people involved.

Pickup lines are lame.

So they can be kind of cute sometimes, but generally they are just pointless and will most likely make people not want to continue the conversation with you. Work on developing some icebreaker statements, but don't use the same one all the time. Change it up so you aren't known as a one trick pony trying to get tricks. Challenge yourself to figure out ways to start conversations that are relevant to your environment and could spur a continued dialogue. Actually, just saying hello and introducing yourself works well as well.

Set yourself up for future encounters.

Sometimes your initial meeting with a new person is just a set up to do something else later. Maybe it is coffee next week or being able to talk to them more at another event.

Friendships can develop over time, so don't think that you need to make concrete plans during your first encounter with someone. Relax and enjoy getting to know them. If there is a positive connection, you will hopefully both make the time to enjoy many fun times together doing a variety of wonderful things.

Sometimes you have to be uncomfortable.

Especially when you are trying to learn something new, you don't look graceful in your execution or feel terribly comfortable doing it. Remember how awkward you felt when you were learning how to ride a bike. Don't be surprised when anxiety rises when you enter a new place or approach someone cute for the first time. It is OK to feel this, but don't let it take over your initiative to talk to someone. Fight through your discomfort and keep working on developing confidence. It should get easier as you gain more experience.

Don't turn yourself down before someone else does.

This is single handedly the biggest mistake many of us make. Just remember that you probably are not psychic and don't necessarily know how someone will respond to you. Don't talk yourself out of going up to someone just because you find them ridiculously good looking. He is not too hot to approach or "out of your league." He may not act like a jackass just because they are attractive. Just talk to him and feel free to mentally refer to the list above if you hit some rough patches.

CHAPTER 5: SELF-IMPROVEMENT

Evolution of the self

Dear Brent,

There are so many parts of myself that I want to be different. I want to lose weight and change the way my body looks, but I also want to date more often and have more sex. It seems like there are things I can do to make myself more attractive to other people, but I want to feel better about myself inside as well so my confidence can increase. Sometimes I just want to start over so people can see a new me without all of their pre-conceived impressions that they have about me now.

Unfortunately entering the witness relocation program to assume a new identity probably isn't an option for you and a sci-fi inspired memory-erasing device hasn't been developed. Many times, a complete make-over is an unrealistic way of looking at how to increase your chances of connecting with others and hopefully you have many positive qualities that you enjoy about yourself. Change generally happens slowly over time and is impacted by working to improve those things about us that cause us high degrees of personal strife. Regardless if it is goals like getting in shape, increasing self-esteem, or becoming better at flirting, getting started and maintaining motivation to keep going can be extremely daunting.

Often when change happens quickly, it is not sustained for a long period of time. We see it most frequently in rapid weight loss when the pounds come off after a fad diet, but come back with a vengeance when we return to our "normally scheduled" behaviors. We may also avoid having to accept that hard work, dedication, and sacrifice may be at the core of creating improved outcomes for us. Taking the easy path is not always the best or most successful route. In addition, running away from things that challenge us may be a natural response, but avoidance doesn't help build the confidence we need to make challenging situations better.

Our lives don't come with a "reset" button and starting completely over isn't often possible. Heading off to college may allow some people to feel that they can shed the stigma of being the awkward geek with no friends, while moving to a new city can give someone confidence that people won't know their sordid past. Regardless, you can't run away from yourself. For all the things we love and dislike about ourselves, the person that looks back at you in the mirror will always be with you. You can run from others, but not from yourself.

Be careful about only focusing on making superficial changes that you think will improve how you feel internally. If only surface changes are made, this new façade needs to be upheld which generally takes lots of energy and focus. Changing in these ways may keep the outside world from perceiving us as a weak and unhappy person, but we will know the truth every time we look at ourselves. This "new and improved" image may seem to look prettier or more socially acceptable, but it is also most likely covering up painful, ugly, or embarrassing parts of us that cause negative effects in our lives and the choices we make.

Although sometimes frustrating or uncomfortable, the process of changing can also be empowering, amazing, and beautiful. Sometimes it progresses slowly and relatively unnoticed. Other times it happens so quickly that we have to put on the breaks to give us a chance to process what is going on. Darwin's theory of evolution has been proven over and over by science and can also be applied to our lives. Thankfully, personal evolution does not need to happen over thousands of years like it does in the animal kingdom.

Strengthening my Resolve

There are times in our lives where it would be nice to have a grab-bag full of strong qualities that could be whipped out when we need them to protect us well when life gets challenging. We would be able to select from a variety of personal strengths that could better equip us to deal with the unexpected or unfortunate situations that can pop up in our lives.

Some of us have a good amount of these at our disposal while others often struggle to get through times when life sucks. Developing these is not only possible, but many times the process of gaining these skills helps us adapt better to situations in the future and increases our confidence overall so we can successfully engage a variety of challenges. This process may be extremely frustrating for some that don't have experience or success in feeling powerful in their own lives, but things can get better as your confidence improves.

Hopefully we develop methods to overcome our past hardships, insecurities, and personal pain. It can be difficult to convince someone that they have the ability to develop qualities like tolerance, self-esteem, hopefulness, or tenacity to accomplish challenging tasks. Fortunately, like many things, these strengths can be learned. It is also important to find those people who can give you suggestions about how to develop skills, support you when you try out new things, and hug you when things don't work out according to your plan. There may be some scrapes and bruises experienced along the way as you learn to navigate the process better, but put on your crash helmet and get ready to start moving.

For those that do not feel like they possess some of these

characteristics so they can begin to gain confidence in taking on challenges, here are a few ways to improve your ability to increase personal strength and confidence. Developing a strong supportive social network is extremely important. It gives us opportunities to reach out when you could use feedback, backup, or a kick in the ass. It also reminds us that we are not alone and have those in our lives who care about our well-being. We also need to take the time to search for the internal and external strengths we already possess, but may have lost touch with due to feeling overwhelmed or beat down. Maybe we have never felt strong or taken opportunities to search internally for what makes us feel confident. Sometimes counselors or close friends are great at helping us see some of those things about us that are out of our line of sight or difficult for us to admit or recognize. This can help us increase our self-awareness and confidence.

Surround yourself with fantastic people. It doesn't matter if that means joining a social group, charitable organization, or hanging out in places where you can make new friends. Working with other people that enjoy fostering a sense of collaboration, teamwork, friendship, and bonding can reinforce the importance of connecting to other people while giving us opportunities to work on communication skills, face our awkwardness, and a reinforce our commitment to working towards enjoying our lives. Through these interactions, we have opportunities to learn how to better increase problem-solving skills and gain confidence that we are capable of changing our own lives.

Many times, the development of these skills is pursued out of a sense of necessity because unfortunate or stressful situations have come into our lives and we need to find methods of coping with them. We can work on ways to adapt to situations, protect ourselves from getting devastatingly hurt, and come out of difficulties with as few abrasions as possible. Working to include qualities like humor, positivity, conviction, empathy, and flexibility into our bag of tricks can help us in developing a strong sense of identity, worthiness, self-esteem, and increase our confidence about bouncing back successfully in spite of life's obstacles.

Don't give up. Find methods to tap into your strengths or take the initiative to identify or create them. Regardless, it takes initiative to incorporate them into our lives. Consider all of the assets we possess that can support the beliefs that we are powerful, driven, and worthy of happiness, success, and love in our lives.

Too hard or not hard enough

There are times when we perceive our life is going in a great direction while during other periods we struggle with feeling defeated, directionless, and like a failure. Personally, I think it is so important to take time out of our busy schedules to do a little hardcore introspection. For some, it is an extremely difficult process that may bring up tons of apprehension, fear, and self-loathing. Others revel in using it as a method to aid them in making their lives better. In our society, some are extremely critical of themselves while others seem to be blissfully unaware that their choices are causing difficulties in their lives.

The process of self-evaluation comes with its own set of emotional challenges. It can also be a scary proposition to look at ourselves because of what we may or may not see. It can trip us up, make us bummed out, or cause us to run away from these realizations while we scream in terror or hopelessness. It can take a lot of courage, energy and focus to engage in this process. We can choose to use our own intelligence, insights and experience, but counting on others to provide additional feedback can be extremely helpful as well. Looking at a reflection of ourselves can be considered a great opportunity to assess where we are in our life journey and use this information to make course corrections or change our direction entirely. It can allow us to figure out our next steps and focus on opportunities to help us attain our goals.

One of the biggest concerns in this process is if we are looking at our qualities in an accurate way or if these aspects of ourselves are being distorted by our own perceptions. We may wonder if we are getting a realistic picture of what is going on or if we are looking at ourselves in the equivalent of a funhouse mirror. There are times when we have all been overly critical in our assessments of ourselves, others in our lives, or situations around us. You may have probably heard of the term "dysmorphia" relating to those who struggle with body image issues that may influence behaviors such as anorexia, bulimia, or steroid abuse. I think the idea can be extended those who have experienced any type of distorted view of ourselves, the world around us, or our place within it. This inaccurate perception can cause us to make unhealthy or unnecessary changes in our lives.

On the flip side, this concept could be applied to some people that often display arrogance, shit-talking, and putting others down. These people may struggle with "kickassery dysmorphia" where it appears that they may think that they are so much more awesome than they really are. Their misguided, incorrect self-assessment has driven them to build an inflated ego. Most often, it is an act to cover up the fact that they have discovered that they feel insecure and experience a lot of shame about themselves. Creating a false front is sometimes a quicker and easier solution for some than taking the time and effort to figure out how to fix the aspects of themselves that they consider broken.

Regardless of what you find when you look at yourself, think about how these parts of you impact your life. There are issues within us that can cause our lives to be feel fun, full and enriched, while other things have the potential to cause high levels of unhappiness including toxic friendships, volatile relationships, and personal anguish. Take the time and effort to see things accurately when we are evaluating ourselves, others, or situations. Don't be scared to look in the mirror and try to see your own true reflection.

Suffering in silence

Many of us have a very hard time asking for help. Sometimes this difficulty may have developed from growing up with a support system that wanted us to handle our own stuff or was absent in our lives when we needed comfort. This may have made us feel they really didn't want to hear about challenges that were stressing us out. There are other families where self-reliance was extremely important or we weren't surrounded by emotionally supportive people. Often, it can be perceived as a positive skill to learn to be self-sufficient and handle a variety of situations happening to us throughout our life, but we can also involve others in this process. In our adulthood, asking for advice or to talk through problems may now feel highly uncomfortable. Many find it difficult to admit when they are really struggling.

We all can benefit from support sometimes and don't have to do everything alone, but it's also not easy to change these old patterns and insecurities.

A very good friend of mine told me about philosophy identifying one of the greatest gifts you could give to someone is the ability to ask for their advice or support. It shows a level of admiration you have for this person since you care enough about their insight, experiences and friendship to ask for their perspective about something you are experiencing. It shows a level of trust to let them know something personal about you, especially when you aren't known for sharing those types of difficulties. This act can also strengthen a relationship between people through getting past difficult situations and building good connections together.

Unfortunately, admitting that we desire assistance, support or a shoulder to cry on could bring up a variety of internal feelings. These may include distrust, self-loathing, insecurity, feeling like a whiny bitch, or not wanting to be seen as a weak person. It could also cause us to experience feelings of anger directed at ourselves for having to ask for help, the situation which is awful enough to make us do it, or other feelings that are brought up deep within us from years of programming and experiences.

In reality, many times we don't want to show our vulnerabilities or perceived weaknesses. They can confirm that we are not the invincible people we market ourselves to be and cause us to question our own strength. When tough times are shared with people we trust, it can reinforce that asking for support is an intelligent and thoughtful way to handle difficult situations - not a sign of weakness.

One difficulty in beginning this process is that it makes us challenge ideas that may have been developed very early in our lives and are often reinforced through our experiences. It is important to begin developing and identifying those relationships we enjoy, but also the ones that allow us to feel comfortable with the level of honesty and trust within it. Some people will focus on being there for their friends, but not using those relationships for support when they need it. It is important to work on asking for support when you really need it. Don't wait until you are at the end of your rope before asking those great friends for help or decide never to use the benefit of their friendship to help you. It may challenge some of our beliefs and require us to swallow our pride and just admit that we don't want or need to do it alone.

It is important to distinguish between when to ask for help and identifying those times when you need to suck it up and deal with something rough. Be conscious about relying too heavily on what other people think or consistently searching for those to support you. While getting help from supportive people in our lives, continue to focus on developing problem-solving skills, tenacity, self-reliance, and the ability to truck forward when situations get rough. Use all your resources to get through challenges when life gets big, bad, and ugly.

Top 10 clichéd phrases that can hurt us

There are many cliché statements out there that have the potential to aid people in feeling like a powerless victim while the world spins around them. Maintaining healthy and positive beliefs about ourselves and our surroundings helps us get up every day ready to engage our lives. Some of these ideas could keep us from searching for things that make us successful and happy. Be careful about using these as an excuse for not getting off your butt and improving your life. Remember, words are powerful and have an impact on us whether thought or spoken. They help us to form helpful or harmful thoughts about ourselves and the world around us.

Time heals all wounds.

Although this can be an important component of getting over the hurt of a situation or a jilted lover, it is important to remember that healing also involves working. Most things don't happen overnight or just because time passes. Don't think that hurt feelings simply resolve themselves. Get off the couch and figure out ways that you can improve situations or fix those things that have caused us difficulty, frustration, or pain.

You can't teach an old dog new tricks.

Sure you can. Actually it doesn't matter how old the dog is, new ways of doing things and expanded visions of their role in the world is always possible. Learning happens throughout our lives. Any established pattern can take time to break or change, but the sooner you begin the process, the sooner it can become replaced with something different that will hopefully benefit your life.

Take the easy way out.

Although this might be a logical way to think, the easy way is not always the most fulfilling way to reach a desired outcome. You may want to look at the most logical solution that will support attaining our goals instead of the easiest option. Be careful about thinking about ways you can get out of putting effort into doing something. It can make us lazy and reinforces the idea that we need to put effort into developing the solution that causes us the least amount of sweat and discomfort instead of the one that can allow for the most personal growth and confidence building.

A good man is hard to find.

There are amazing people out there. The biggest trick is to find them and recognize them when they are in front of your face. It is important to put yourself out there to increase your chances of connecting. After that, do things that allow for opportunities to get to know people. Whether you connect face-to-face or if they are a cyber-buddy, challenges can exist in seeing them as a person that can enrich your life. Open your eyes because there are probably some amazing people right in front of you.

Better safe than sorry.

Sometimes playing it safe keeps us from trying something that we might not do well. We might also be scared that we will fail in the execution. Some of the greatest accomplishments happen after we have fallen down a few times. Crying a bit, putting on the Band-Aid, and working to get better at doing something builds character and increases our confidence that we can accomplish it.

Life's a bitch.

This way of thinking can keep us from looking beyond how cranky we feel about some crap-tastic situations in our lives. I think it's better to think that life can just be difficult at times. Keep in mind that puppies are cute, tiramisu tastes incredible, free will is awesome, and life is really an amazing gift.

You can't fit a square peg in a round hole.

Although this is true, there are some holes that are really fun to stretch out. Many times people think that situations are the wrong size, just way too big, or couldn't possibly fit in that snug hole that represents our current life. Somehow with the right angle, lubrication, and perseverance, we can get it in. Stop thinking about situations so rigidly. There are ways to make almost any circumstance work out. Our perception that we don't fit in or have no ability to make certain situations work causes feelings of powerlessness when we could spend time attempting to solve the problem.

The best things in life are free.

Of course some things are considered free while others come at a great price. For those things that take time, effort, compromise, and sweat to accomplish, the payoffs can be quite amazing. Expecting things to be free or easy can make us feel entitled to receive more than we deserve or for things to come to us effortlessly.

Love is blind.

It doesn't have to be. This is a statement that assumes that you won't see concerning behaviors in your partner when you're in love. You can see the approaching train or listen for the chugging. It's important to be aware and acknowledge when that little voice in your head says "run." Most times we see the danger coming, but choose to ignore it or stick with it in hopes that it is going to change.

It is what it is.

This is what people say about situations that they feel are out of their control and suck really badly. Not only does this reinforce that you are powerless, but also that things will continue to be really bad until they spontaneously turn around on their own and get better. We can have an impact on many things. Try to find ways to decrease the negative impact of those frustrating issues that we can't change and focus on all the other things we can impact positively.

The importance of the journey

Dear Brent,

I have had a history of working really hard to reach a particular goal in my life and then quickly move on to the next task at hand. Many people have told me that I don't take the time to enjoy my successes or feel pride about how much effort it took to reach my goals. I personally don't think it's necessary for me to sit back and waste time reveling in my accomplishments. How would doing that benefit me and why would I need to change my patterns?

It sounds like some people may be concerned you are not fully appreciating your efforts in achieving positive things in your life. Some of us appear to be singularly focused on attaining a goal as quickly as possible with as little resistance and effort necessary to reach it. Very few of us want to work harder than we need to, but rushing to get things done may come with a set of unique pitfalls. You don't necessarily have to change the ways you go after your goals, but there are some things to consider.

There is a big difference between running from project to project as quickly as possible and resting too long on your successes, patting yourself incessantly on the back, and waiting for the adoration from others to make you feel great about your accomplishments.

Take a moment and think about the road you must travel to successfully achieve something. Figuring out a personal desire, developing a well-crafted plan, showing the perseverance to continue fighting when things get challenging, and eventually emerging triumphant based on your efforts are all aspects we may experience when working to reach a goal. We face challenges and our own insecurities while forging ahead and may need to develop different methods to achieve what we want. All of these things take creativity, strength, and heart.

Many feel that we may benefit more from the process of

working to reach a goal or achieve something than simply the enjoyment of attaining it. In many ways, the process we go through in working to gain various successes can enrich our lives more than just the delight of sweet victory. The emotional elation, self-esteem and confidence building, and desire to run around getting high-fives from your buddies are just a few of the benefits of allowing ourselves to take the time to reflect on our achievements.

You don't have to take weeks out of your schedule to search for people to get excited for you, but maybe a few moments, hours, or days to allow yourself to celebrate in your own success can increase your own feelings of happiness regarding your achievements.

Even though you may have a lot on your plate, running from task to task quickly isn't always necessary. Taking this time to evaluate the process and enjoy our successes can have a significant impact on our lives. It is so much more than simply counting how many things we can achieve or how many times we can win. It speaks to our ability to remain strong in the face of difficulties, change our course or tactics when necessary, overcome situations that can be painful or frustrating, and develop the confidence that we can get those things we truly want through perseverance and hard work.

Thankfully life doesn't always need to parallel a mad dash on Black Friday to get a killer deal. There are times when slowing down to experience situations from a different perspective or evaluate things more closely can really benefit us. It's fine to be delighted about the efforts we have put into getting what we want, but also don't spend too much time prancing around like a proud peacock. Take the time to enjoy your victory, get some rest, and then prepare for the set of adventures to tackle.

Top 10 clichéd phrases that can benefit us

Although using clichés can be seen as taking the easy way

out when giving advice or offering support, there can also be truth found deep within them. Consider how these common phrases can be applied in your efforts to improve your life.

Hindsight is 20/20.

Of course it is. There is no challenge in picking this week's lotto numbers after they have been announced. Since you can't go back in time, when you experience those learning moments where the outcome of a situation smacks you upside your head, file these memories away in your "woulda-shoulda-coulda" file for next time you experience something similar and do it differently next time.

Beauty is in the eye of the beholder.

So true, but we have to stop thinking that we know what the beholder is thinking. Don't waste energy in making up reasons for why someone wouldn't be attracted or interested in you. Everyone has different qualities they look for in friends, dates and partners. There is more to being attractive than a chiseled jawline and ripped abs. Focus on developing things that make you proud and confident, then work on discovering people that appreciate them.

Just breathe.

Take a moment and take in few deep ones. Many times when we get overwhelmed or stressed, our breathing gets more shallow and rapid. Taking a few moments to inhale some deep breaths oxygenates the blood, but also gives us an opportunity to chill out for a moment and get our thoughts calmed down. Think about another cliché phrase, "in with the good, out with the bad." Work on blowing out the negativity and replacing it with confidence.

Make it work.

This may have been made popular by Tim Gunn from the television show "Project Runway," but it is important to remember that there are times where failure isn't a good option and definitely not one that you want to make. The task may benefit from you stepping outside your comfort zone and trying something new. It may also require you to complete the task in a different way than you would in a perfect world.

It's progress, not perfection.

This famous Alcoholics Anonymous quote is about moving forward toward a goal without the importance of accomplishing it perfectly right now. Don't worry about getting it absolutely 100 percent right at this time. Stop using the fear of failure to keep you from trying something. Continue your attempts to get better or improve your situation. You will gain more confidence with your ability to make progress than if you wait to feel good about yourself for doing it completely perfectly.

Suck it up.

This is also known as "put on your Big Girl Panties and deal with it." There are times in our lives that we just have to acknowledge that a situation is going to be difficult or suck. The longer we put it off or stress about how we don't want to do it, the better possibility we have to not complete the task or make it more intimidating than it needs to be. Many times, the anticipation is worse than actually just doing it.

Don't judge a book by its cover.

It's unfortunate that people judge others before taking the time to get to know their personalities, passions, strengths and quirks. It's good to remember that most of us are not psychic and need to challenge ideas about what we think we know about others. We may be surprised by what we discover.

Get a life.

Seriously, find one! Take the time to discover those things that interest and intrigue us. Pursue those situations that can make our lives feel more fulfilled and eventful. Hold onto those people that turn us on and make us smile.

Nothing ventured, nothing gained.

If fear of failure wasn't a factor, we would all probably engage with some things differently. Approach situations with positive amounts of courage and confidence without concerns about what happens when you don't do it as well as you want to. Challenge yourself to practice those things that you want to improve. Like they say, "dance like there is no one watching you."

Actions are more important than words.

Talk can definitely be cheap and a person's actions speak to their integrity and strength of character. This belief can be beneficial in many ways including building honest relationships and reinforcing responsible living. Be a person of your word and not someone that talks out of their ass or doesn't follow through. It's important to remember that "playing" a good game is much more important than "talking" a good game.

Does it really get better?

Columnist Dan Savage and his partner Terry Miller are credited with being the powerful force behind the "It Gets Better" campaign that brought awareness to the bullying and depression problems of LGBTQ youth. Their efforts have driven home the point that queer youth do not need to feel alone in their struggles and their lives will get better as long as they can get through their difficult adolescent years. Unfortunately for many, happiness and fulfillment still hasn't been found as they get older.

In addition to telling people not to give up, we must instill hope that life can improve for us because we do things to change it. Life definitely isn't easy. Even without feeling bullied, many of us have struggled with low self-esteem, fear of rejection from our loved ones, feeling undesirable, or seeing ourselves as less worthy then our straight counterparts. This may come from listening to rhetoric from particular members of the press, politicians, religious leaders, family and friends. Regardless, these messages can be very damaging.

Hurtful interactions throughout our lives bruise us emotionally and can lead to depression, isolation, substance abuse, destructive behaviors, and unfortunately suicide. We can feel beat down and trapped which influences us to stay in bad relationships, hate our bodies, and deal with stressful situations in unhealthy ways. We can wait, hope, or pray that these things will get better, but we need to take steps to actively create opportunities to help ourselves. There is never going to be a perfect time to start working on things, so we need to stop waiting for planets to align and start making deliberate moves.

We face challenges daily and it generally takes more to overcome them than just waiting for it to get better. Very few things in our lives are certain. You may receive a fortune from a cookie after a great Chinese lunch that states "you will achieve great wealth and success." If you sit on your ass for the next 20 years waiting for the enchanted million-dollar check to arrive, you will most likely be disappointed as well as homeless. Similarly, ignoring problems rarely makes them go away. Even if feelings pass, they will most likely re-emerge again.

It doesn't matter whether you're a kid or a prime-timer, if you who are struggling with feelings of rejection, hopelessness, or desperation, it is important to hang in and keep fighting. There will always be aspects that we want to improve, insecurities that surface and challenges for us to face. Focus on developing qualities like compassion, honesty and integrity. Develop true self-esteem by taking the time to discover your passions and interests. Don't be so worried about fitting into some mold so you will be accepted. There is nothing wrong with being different.

Take opportunities to increase personal strengths like your intellect and perseverance while accomplishing things that set yourself up for long-term success. Being patient is also extremely important. You usually don't get buff after working out for only a month or find Prince Charming while hanging out in a bar occasionally. If you want to get in shape, then it's important to make healthier food decisions and work out. If you are looking for a man that makes your heart flutter, spend time figuring out what you want in a relationship and develop skills to talk to people. Usually things get better because we have put the sweat and effort into making them better.

Great things can take a chunk of time to achieve, so be careful about developing frustration, anger, and resentment when things don't happen as quickly or easily as you hoped. These feelings can have a severe negative impact on your motivation to keep working towards these goals. Don't become discouraged about how long it will take or scared about how difficult the process will be.

Many of us focus primarily on achieving an end goal and getting there as quickly and easily as possible. The process of reaching that destination is often much more important than rushing blindly towards the finish line. Although challenging, it can help us develop the confidence that we can handle adversity. We all possess the potential to create an amazing life full of great relationships, happiness, and prosperity.

Work to achieve those things that improve your quality of life and make you a better person. Challenge yourself to heal those aspects of yourself that have been bruised by your experiences instead of working hard to cover them up. Find the internal motivation and supportive people to help you on your journey. It's OK to ask for help when you need it. Don't wait for it to get better, develop the strength and skills to make it better.

Realizations from my decade of growth

So many of us want to improve our lives, increase our chances to connect with great people, and wake up each day with renewed excitement to get out of bed and attack the day. Having a desire to work on self-improvement is fantastic, but without a plan and the energy to put these changes into motion, all the daydreams in the world won't do anything to create differences in our lives. It can be extremely hard to get the ball rolling. Here are some realizations that I have come to understand that will hopefully benefit you as much as they have helped me.

I can be my own best friend or worst enemy.

In our lives, we can act as our own biggest supporter or an extremely abusive bully, sometimes both depending on the situation. It is so important to be aware of how we perceive ourselves and what our internal voice says about us when we look at the mirror. Self-deprecation and a lack of self-esteem is a huge detriment in creating a great life. We have the ability to be much crueler and destructive to ourselves than others may be to us. Unfortunately these negative self-perceptions can permeate many parts of our lives and impact our ability to accomplish our goals. When we are feeling confident and powerful about ourselves, our ability to move forward seems more possible with less difficulties. Fabricating our own barriers keeps us from working toward creating improvements in our lives and reinforces feelings of being ineffective in making these changes.

My desires are not something to feel guilty about.

Shame has been such a large part of many of our lives growing up and unfortunately has latched onto our adult lives. It is hard enough to allow ourselves to figure out what really fulfills us physically, emotionally, spiritually, and sexually without having ourselves try to stomp it out instead of supporting our enjoyment. Feeling confident and proud of who we are is integral in our personal development into a person we truly appreciate. Stop apologizing for aspects of ourselves that we enjoy.

I can change my situation.

Almost anything can be worked on or improved. Feeling trapped in any situation reinforces feelings of powerlessness and demotivates us to get off our asses to make changes. Working to identify those issues that we have the ability to change in our lives makes us feel stronger and more confident overall. Finding the focus and motivation is also key in this process. Don't get trapped in thinking that you are a victim of your circumstances. You have the ability, now find the focus, desire, and energy to work on it.

Family is important.

In addition to being raised by biological parents, there are many of us that have been supported by extended family members, neighbors, friends, and other extremely influential people in our lives. Hold on to them and express your appreciation and affection for them as much as possible. Being surrounded with love is what makes life fulfilling.

The world does not have to be a hostile place.

Getting up every day thinking that we are going to be attacked or have a metaphorical bird poop on us can increase feelings of paranoia and a sense of impending doom. This can stop us from recognizing amazing people and opportunities around us. Having this attitude may make us appear like a grumpy, self-loathing downer that will pull the good mood out of any enjoyable situation. The longer this belief exists in our lives, the more difficult it can be to see the world in a positive light. Our environment is much easier to deal with when we work on seeing the beauty around us instead of focusing on everything that is wrong.

Courage is crucial.

Quit being so afraid. It is hard to convince someone that they don't need to be fearful of rejection or failure, but they need to get over it. Although disappointment sucks, it happens to everyone at one time or another. Avoiding the possibility of defeat can keep you from feeling its painful sting, but most times it also keeps you from participating in life. Trying something new isn't bad. Don't be upset if you don't master the process during your first attempt.

Good people are great to find.

Take the time to work on connecting with as many incredible people as possible. It may seem elusive at times, but they are absolutely out there. Sometimes just being open to finding them is one of the most helpful aspects of connecting with others. Don't assume that you know how every situation will play out and you may have to take a chance to see what happens. They don't all have to be your best friend, but having people around can give you support when faced with a rough situation or an extra pair of hands to move that awkward sofa.

Confidence is sexy.

Insecurity definitely is not an attractive quality and is especially ugly when it is saved for the barstool or a first date. When you walk into a room, stand up straight and walk tall. If you are in a low self-esteem mindset, you are not going to come across to anyone as potentially interesting, charismatic, or confident. Discussing how a person is too attractive to be talking to you or how you hate your body is a horrible waste of time and energy while also making you look totally tragic. If someone gives you a compliment, for God's sake, just say, "thank you."

Don't judge a book by it's over.

Try not to let your own insecurities influence your thoughts about someone you haven't taken the opportunity to get to know yet. Chances are that you are not psychic and may be pleasantly surprised that someone may not live up to the negative impression of how you imagine them. Our own insecurities can sometimes be projected onto other people and make them appear quite unattractive. Take the time to get to know someone instead of assuming that you instinctively know all of their character defects. Don't assume that they will be a jerk just because you find them attractive or you perceive them as being popular. Most people out there really are nice.

Be true to yourself and those around you.

Integrity is one of the few items in our lives that we have almost completely within our control. What comes out of your mouth and what you do with your time and body is up to you. Live up to your own potential and follow through with what you promise to yourself and others. Don't focus on what you think you need to be doing to make other people like and accept you. It's more important to find those who love us for all of our strengths, quirks, and follies.

CHAPTER 6: RELATIONSHIPS

What is commitment?

With gay marriage as a new reality for many in our community, it has encouraged conversations for some of us about how we want to live within the context of having a committed relationship, including how it may be perceived and valued by others. There is nothing in the rule book that says that any of us have to conform to a single set of predetermined structures or expectations. It doesn't have to mirror stereotypical "straight" versions that many of us grew up seeing. Ward and June Cleaver don't need to be the picture of our desired relationship or perfect marriage.

As increasingly diverse types of relationships begin to become more common in our community, the definitions of particular words may also need to evolve as well. The terminology used to describe commitment, fidelity, or faithfulness in a relationship today may differ from what was considered appropriate previously. In the past, it may have appeared to be much more straight-forward.

Although not all types of relationships are tantalizing for all people, it is very important to remember that each person in the arrangement should feel comfortable with the dynamics and confident in their ability to play by their agreed rules.

What one couple may consider "cheating" could be a perfectly acceptable practice for others. Every relationship has its own set of expectations. Fidelity is all about sticking to your agreements and being honest. These relationship rules may or may not include who or how you interact with others in physically or emotionally intimate ways. Infidelity or cheating in a relationship can be considered something as direct as screwing someone else or having what would be deemed as an inappropriate exchange. It is truly up to the individuals involved to decide.

Keep in mind is that everything in a partnership is potentially open to discussion and can also be subject to change. If a trial experiment fails, hopefully the core of any relationship is a deep-rooted trust, love, and loyalty that can get you through rough circumstances. This strong foundation will hopefully also translate into having the confidence to discuss desires and concerns with your partner without fear of a Chernobyl-esque disaster that ends the relationships.

Activities only need to be considered cheating or inappropriate if they break the rules between people. This is why it is so important to take the time to figure out what each person wants in a relationship and be honest, thoughtful, and authentic when it comes to expressing those to each other. Relationship agreements need to be shared, discussed, and understood between the people involved. Unfortunately, many times individuals feel uncomfortable or insecure about expressing what they really desire within the arrangement and choose to just do what they want behind their partner's back.

Each participant's integrity is of extremely high importance. This quality includes doing the right thing when no one else is looking over your shoulder or because there is a low chance of getting caught doing the wrong thing. Additionally, both partners should feel validated, supported, and excited about the agreements. We are all adults and can make decisions that are right for us as well as having our wants and needs fulfilled without cheating, lying, or manipulating. Every relationship has the potential to be meaningful and beautiful. It can also be destroyed by assumptions, poor communication, insecurities, or being a low-down, sneaky bastard that breaks the rules to selfishly get his own needs met at the expense of his partner's well-being and the eventual demise of the relationship.

In a world of increasing acceptance for a wide variety of relationships, the only rules that truly matter are the ones developed by those involved within it. As long as your relationship is strong, it shouldn't matter how it is composed or what the terms of engagement are. Just remember to show respect, love, and commitment to each other.

Is my new relationship a priority?

Dear Brent,

I met a guy online and we hit it off. We like hanging out with each other. It's amazing how much we have in common and how much we seem to just enjoy each other's company. I am unfortunately seeing some patterns emerge that are concerning to me. He forgets things or doesn't follow through with promises he makes. He also sometimes blows me off to hang out with other people. I have been careful not to put too much pressure on him, but his lack of follow through frustrates me and I'm feeling that our relationship may not be a high priority for him or might be dating around with other people without telling me. I don't know if he is really this absent minded or he is just not that serious about me. What do you think I should do?

If you're concerned that he isn't being honest with you about his activities, turning into a psycho gay stalker that hides in bushes acting like a private investigator trying to snap pictures of him in inappropriate activities would be a negative way to pursue this relationship. If you are feeling like that is becoming a good possibility for you, it is definitely time to take a step back and regroup. Those kinds of attitudes don't benefit anyone and it will eventually cause a blow up. If you want him to live up to the expectations he has promised you, then that is a totally reasonable reason to be voicing concern. It is perfectly understandable to become disappointed or angry at someone that doesn't follow through.

My first suggestion to anyone who complains about someone upsetting them is to talk to them directly about it. Many people will grumble about how they feel hurt or irritated by someone's actions, but they haven't communicated this to the other person so it can be discussed or corrected. It's hard for people to identify a problem if they don't know that one exists in the first place. It is important to make sure that your concerns are communicated so the other person understands how you are feeling and what you hope will change in the future.

There is nothing wrong with expecting someone to remember plans made with you or to hold them accountable when they don't follow through with them. Sometimes people may not realize their actions have negative impacts on others or how it affects you emotionally. The possibility may exist that his memory really sucks or does not take the time to schedule commitments on his calendar. Regardless, we are all adults and responsible for being where we are supposed to be at the scheduled time and to follow through with our word.

Compatibility in a relationship exists on many levels. It sounds like you are thinking there is potential for this relationship to move forward in a deeper way. Make sure you are both perceiving the relationship in similar ways.

There can be times where two individuals may have a differed perception of the same relationship. In these kinds of situations, one may think that the interaction is a lot of fun and the sex makes him want to do a victory lap around the bedroom while the other person may be laying there in afterglow thinking about what their relationship may look like five years down the road while they are on a trip to Berlin. Having awareness of both people's desires and perceptions is extremely important to reduce the possibility of misunderstanding or hurt feelings.

You may want to ask him if he is feeling any long-term relationship potential between the two of you. Be aware that you may get an answer that you don't want to hear, but it is better to have a firm understanding of how each of you is seeing your relationship and potentially setting some new ground rules for how you schedule time together. I would encourage anyone to bring up relationship concerns as soon as possible before resentment builds up too much. Having positive open communication where both people feel that they are being heard is a cornerstone of any healthy relationship regardless if you are getting naked or not. Don't sweep this under the carpet and hope that it will get better.

I'm mistrusting my new relationship

Dear Brent,

I have been dating a great guy for several weeks and we are serious about each other. We both agreed that for right now we want to be monogamous, but we have discussed opening it up somewhat in the future. I discovered that there are two guys my boyfriend often communicates with and talks about finding time to meet up. We have discussed being honest and he claims that he is still being faithful. I don't want to lose my guy, but I'm seeing some red flags. What would you do?

It sounds like you both recognize that rolling around naked with just one person for the rest of your relationship may not be one of your long-term relationship goals. It also doesn't sound like you trust that he is being honest with you about his potential sexual activities when meeting up with guys. I would question if you just don't trust him or if your perceptions have been tainted to not trust any gay dude that you are dating when he hangs out with other gay guys. There is the old adage that "boys will be boys" and can be applied to some people's opinion that gay men are unable to be dedicated, faithful, or honest. Other people are just simply cheaters.

Trust can be one of those things that builds up over time, but hopefully you are a good judge of character and have chosen someone that has integrity. Unfortunately, there are those people that lie, cheat, and sneak around. There are also some of us that have done that in the past to other people and in relationships. These types of situations in our histories can make us feel insecure and look for "X-Files" conspiracy theories within relationships.

Before you hire a private investigator to lurk in the bushes while he takes pictures of your boyfriend's coffee date, take the time to talk to him about your personal concerns and where they come from. A relationship that is not built on trust is absolutely doomed to fail. If you care about continuing to form a strong bond with him, take the time and effort to have conversations about a variety of things you want out of a relationship and expectations you have for each other. These include passions, insecurities, pet peeves, dreams, and concerns.

I'm curious about what conversations you have had with your boyfriend around his activities with these guys. The process of "meeting up" can be something as innocent as grabbing a bite with old buddies. It could also be that they are planning on getting freaky. Regardless if they have bent each other over in the past or not, gay men can develop non-sexual friendships with each other. Although some feel that this species of monogamous and trustworthy homo is rare or extinct, they do exist in nature.

Another pitfall that some couples experience is thinking that your world needs to revolve around that super awesome person that you just started dating. In the honeymoon period, you can't get enough of each other, text 200 times a day while you're at work reminding each other how much you are yearning for their touch, and spend every available moment together. Maintaining contact with old friends and having separate interests can be a really healthy part of getting into a committed relationship.

Seven deadly sins in relationships

Although many of us love the idea of bathing in a sea of excess, these cardinal sins can cause significant upheaval in our lives and have the potential to tear apart meaningful interactions with others. Not only can these serve to weaken and destroy romantic relationships, but may also has a profoundly negative impact on our enjoyment of our interactions with other people. These sins cause dysfunction in people's lives and reinforce that our relationships are chaotic, unfulfilling, and tragic. Beware when these sinful behaviors begin to take over your relationships.

Wrath

Feeling scorned can be awful, but it can cause negative perspectives about the world and its inhabitants. This may lead someone into lashing out at others and can also be quite addictive. So many people in our community live in a place of frustration, anger, and bitterness. Not only can this turn people away from wanting to spend time with us, but reinforces that we are surrounded by storm clouds just waiting to screw up our day.

Greed

There are absolutely times where we want to focus primarily on our own desires. This could also be perceived as extremely selfish and may signal that we are trying to make up for a lack of fulfillment internally. For some, achieving their desires may mean keeping secrets, going behind someone's back, or dismissing other's wishes to get their own needs met. Be cautious of stepping on the backs of our friends to get what we want.

Sloth

This can look many different ways in our relationships. It may happen when we don't address issues that tend to fester and may blow up in our faces if not discussed. We may drag our feet with situations that may be confrontational or make us feel uncomfortable.

Pride

As we challenge our own ideas of self-worth and lower self-esteem, it can be easy to move to a place of over-compensation. This may also happen with building up a false persona to show power instead of finding confidence in ourselves. It can also stop us from asking for help when we could benefit from it and choose to handle situations on our own.

Lust

Of all of these sins, this is the most fun and exciting for most of us. It can be so easy to get wrapped up in because the feelings for another person can be incredibly intense. Hopefully we are fortunate enough to cross paths with those who bring up feelings of passion and connection. These people will also hopefully make particular body parts swell and allow our minds to wonder about future possibilities. Unfortunately this can cause us to lose focus on important parts of our lives like friendships and other responsibilities.

Envy

It's not unusual to want things, but if we spend our energy focusing on being jealous of what we perceive others have in their lives, we don't enjoy our own path of trying to shape our lives in meaningful ways. Not only can our perception be wrong about other people and what they have, but it makes us focus on what we don't have and our deficits.

Gluttony

Too much is never enough! It is natural to want more of a good thing, but we all know what can happen when we overeat at buffets. Regardless if we are talking about hooking up, partying, having fun, shopping, or getting obsessed over the hottest new fad, this can cause us to get wrapped up a single focus that may keep us from engaging in the rest of our life. Sometimes moderation is a good thing.

What should I do about by chubby partner?

Dear Brent,

My long-time partner has been gaining a lot of weight in the past few years and it's getting harder for me to stay sexually interested in him. He complains about my lack of sex drive sometimes, but I'm just not attracted to him with his extra weight. One night he caught me masturbating on the couch after I snuck out of the bed to get off. He got up to pee and saw me, and now he's really angry because it was just an hour after I told him that I was not feeling horny. I don't think I can avoid the issue anymore. How do you suggest I deal with this?

We all change over time in a variety of ways, regardless if it is with our physical appearance, interests, family issues, health concerns, or life choices. When we are in committed relationships, there are times when our partner changes in ways that may not be pleasing to us. For that matter, sometimes we can change in ways we are not happy with either. We might not like ourselves totally when we stare into the mirror. The reflection may not currently be the fairest of them all like it was at earlier points in our lives. Additionally, the phrase "love is blind" is not always true. We are aware of things that cause us to lose interest or be concerned.

Body shape is one of those things that tends to fluctuate often over time. Our focus and interest in maintaining an eye-catching physique can decrease as we get more comfortable in our relationship or focused on other things. Life can definitely get in the way of some of our fitness goals. Like with any situation where resentment, dissatisfaction, or a lack of honest communication are present, this could serve to help destroy your relationship. It does seem like you are going to have to address this issue relatively soon instead of putting it off or lying about your concern.

Sexual interest generally tends to go up and down in relationship, but can absolutely be negatively impacted by each partner's physical attraction to each other. It doesn't sound like you are just putting your feelings and concerns directly on the table. I'm assuming that part of you is concerned about hurting his feelings, but there is also most likely a part that doesn't want to have this discussion because it is an uncomfortable confrontation. There are only so many times where you can claim to have a headache or pretend to be sleeping. Although being honest about your feelings may cause hurt feelings, at least you are being honest with him.

Your subtle clues may also be too subtle. There are times where hints may be perceived as simply chitchat or off-handed comments. You could offer support by suggesting that both of you to begin eating better and getting in shape. You could take the initiative to begin going to the gym or coming home from work and cooking a healthier meal. This may be a good time to stop thinking about how unhappy you are with the situation and take steps to begin having a positive impact on it. He could recognize your progress and dedication to healthier living which could have a positive impact on him doing similar things or taking the initiative to make some of his own changes.

Couples can get very comfortable in their relationship and easily fall into ruts. If you have been together for a long time, hopefully you have established a strong foundation of respect and love between both of you. This can be a strong ally when having these types of difficult conversations. They aren't brought up to be judgmental or mean-spirited. Sit down with each other and have a conversation about where both of you are in the context of this relationship and what you hope to see in the future. I'm curious to hear if your partner is as attracted to you as he was when you first started dating. There may be aspects of you that your partner is not feeling as excited about either.

Married straight homosexual searching for answers

Dear Brent,

I'm in a long-term heterosexual relationship, but I am a gay man. I finally gave into my urges and have been playing around on my wife with guys for the past year. I'm in a profession that I don't think will accept me if I come out and our children and friends would absolutely hate me for lying to them. I feel that keeping it secret is going to be my best option, but I hate sneaking around and feel really guilty. Do you have any advice for me?

I think you are 100 percent right. Sneaking around and lying to people in your life is the best option for you to maintain your double life. We have all had the opportunity to see the fall of the mighty "straight-acting," phony-heterosexual homo who gets caught soliciting sex in an airport bathroom or cheats on his wife in sleazy hotel rooms while getting cracked out, rubbed down, and sucked off. Based on the history of many gay married men before you, you are well on your way to getting caught. For most people it is just a matter of time.

You are faced with a difficult decision to possibly come out on your own terms or wait until a situation happens that could force you out of the closet screaming in terror.

I appreciate it can be difficult to be honest with yourself and to other people around you, especially about sexuality. I think that almost everyone has felt insecure about their sexuality at various times in their lives. It is especially not unusual for people that are attracted to others of the same sex to feel scared that they are not part of the majority, face potential negative judgment, and could be the target of violence or aggression. Most of us get to the point that being honest about our attractions overshadows these fears and we begin the process of coming out to our friends and family, and most importantly to ourselves. I would like to think that our culture is becoming generally more accepting of gay individuals, but some people continue to struggle with feelings that acceptance from others will not happen.

I'm curious about how much sex you have with your wife. If you identify as a homosexual, I can only assume that you feel that your primary sexual attraction is to males. Following this logic to a strong possible conclusion, you are most likely not into sexual contact with your wife which would suggest that she is not being sexually satisfied by you. In changing the focus from you to her for a moment, realize that she is most likely not getting the physical pleasure she could receive by someone who actually wants to see her naked. I personally don't feel that it is fair that you are getting your rocks off while your wife sits at home waiting for you to finish up with your undisclosed "man date" with a buddy.

I'm going to stick my neck out there and publicly state that cheating is never an acceptable option. It doesn't matter if you identify as gay, straight, closeted, or "not gay but enjoys pounding man butt." You can try to justify that cheating is OK because your partner doesn't understand you, give you what you need, or is a woman and you're a big poofter. In the end, it doesn't matter. Grow a pair and either figure out how to improve your relationship or end it. It is not fair to your partner to keep those things from her.

There is absolutely no way that you can continue to get what you want physically from a man and maintain any personal integrity about your actions. You are purely focused on what you want, regardless of the impact on other people, especially your wife. Be cautious about stating that you are keeping these secrets for the benefit of your friends and family. I think it is poor justification for being a liar.

Historically gay men and straight women make fantastic pairs for ice skating, shopping buddies, watching the Oscars, or dishing about stupid males. Homos generally make really awful husbands for women, especially when the wife doesn't don't know that they are homos. If you truly love her, consider the importance of both of you getting what each of you need in the relationship. Honesty and respect are two of the most important tenants we can promise to anyone. Our personal integrity is one of the few things we have complete control over in our lives. I think it may be time to take a long hard look in the mirror and decide what type of man you are.

A player's game

Dear Brent,

I started posting profiles on gay networking and hookup sites about a year ago and told my partner that I was using them to chat with old friends and meet new people. I started meeting some of these guys for coffee or lunch during the day, but it's progressed to hooking up with some of them for the past few months. I love my partner, but he would completely freak out and break up with me if he found out. I really enjoy these daytime hookups, but I don't want to end my relationship.

It can definitely suck when the brain that resides in the male penis takes over the logic produced by the brain that lives in our other head. Cheating is cheating regardless of how much you love your partner or want to stay in the relationship. That being said, your situation brings up some other questions.

I'm curious if your initial intention about posting profiles on these sites was solely based on making friendships. Don't get me wrong, people have forged extremely strong relationships with people met online and it can be used for much more than just hooking up for sex. Having an online presence is a fantastic way to market yourself in many ways. Some are on there for hooking up, while others are searching for activity partners and new friends. Sometimes they are interested in all of those things. You would have to do some soul searching to figure out why you began posting profiles in the first place. It may be possible that you were looking for some kind of excitement or fulfillment that you weren't getting in your relationship or had the intention of looking for opportunities to cheat on your partner.

It is very easy to fall into something called "pre-cheating." This is where you start dipping your big toe in the pool to check the temperature before jumping into the water. For some, this is a seemingly non-threatening way to start checking out who else is out there and if they would be interested in meeting up with you without leaving the safety of a relationship. There is not much of a leap between a little sexy talk online and moving that to physical contact sometimes. Some people really do enjoy the online chat as a way to get to know people and extend their circle of friends, while others use it for some kind of cyber-sexual exchange. Being turned on by hot talk is normal, but doing these activities can definitely cause desires to increase and can set you up to get in trouble.

If you are pursuing these opportunities and it is not within the boundaries of your relationship, you may want to take a hard look at what you want in your relationship and how your choices have the potential to destroy it. Some people try to supplement areas of their relationships that are not working instead of putting the effort into fixing these. In healthy, balanced relationships, partners are getting what they want physically, sexually, emotionally and socially. Of course it is unrealistic to think that one person can be completely fulfilling to someone in all areas, but honesty about what is not being fulfilled is important to be communicated.

There may also be a possibility that your partner could be interested in messing around with other people as well. I'm assuming by the language in your question, you have not taken the opportunity to discuss modifying your relationship to allow for you both to hook up with other people. Most times, relationships change over time in various ways. People find new interests and passions while some things you both used to enjoy can get boring. There is nothing philosophically wrong with wanting to be sexual with multiple people, just as long as honesty exists between all parties involved. Maybe this kind of contact is something you can share with your partner, together or separately. Adding new sexual elements isn't necessarily a bad thing in a relationship.

At this point, your actions are absolutely selfish. This is all about your personal desires. You are maintaining the appearance of monogamy with your partner and friends while getting your rocks off with someone else. Not only are you disrespecting your partner and the relationship, but they are also denying your partner the opportunity to make some choices for himself, including if he wants to re-evaluate some relationship boundaries or stay with you. Sounds like you have a potentially difficult conversation ahead of you.

Fifty shades of cheating

In our current world full of diversity, relationships can be constructed in a variety of ways, paired with their own unique set of rules, expectations, and understandings. For individuals involved in any type of relationship, the importance of defining agreements and the degree to which all involved participants follow through with them will have the most impact on how successful the relationship most likely will be. Put simply, make the rules and follow them. One of the most important aspects to figure out will be to determine what constitutes cheating and to build that trust within the relationship to help lessen the potential for jealousy, accusations, and hurt feelings.

Regardless if the relationship is monogamous or open, there are interactions with others that may be considered inappropriate. It is massively important to sit down, figure out which expectations are important, and communicate them with those people involved in the relationship. This is not a conversation where only one person's perspective matters. Compromises may need to be made or the reality of irreconcilable differences may need to be addressed. Not every relationship is destined to work out and your current Prince Charming may simply be a great guy who needs to be sent back into the magical forest to wait for someone who is more compatible. Be careful that everyone involved in this relationship venture is in agreement and is as supportive as possible. Those who feel backed into a corner or who have to sacrifice a core part of their belief system can become angry, withdrawn, or decide to say screw it and do whatever they want. Hopefully everyone is happy with the agreement and can whole-heartedly agree to uphold it.

Each relationship has its own base philosophies. Monogamy works for many people, but they may also utilize the belief that those who "play together, stay together" where they can discuss other expectations for when they may bring other people into their bedroom. For the non-monogamous versions, some feel that a "don't ask, don't tell" policy works for them or they may adopt the "please tell me every detail because it really turns me on to know that you're having a sweaty damn good time" method of communication. Each relationship is a unique situation composed of different activities and understandings. Some relationships are best friends, but not necessarily interested in pursuing all of the same interests. Others could be considered almost carbon copies of each other. Regardless, most successful relationships are forged with high levels of loyalty and respect.

Over time, relationships tend to adjust and evolve, which can cause permutations from the original version. This is a natural progression that should not be seen as necessarily unhealthy. It can however be challenging for the people involved. Hopefully we all have the desire and opportunity to transform throughout our lives and in our relationships. This may also change the definition of how we define cheating. It is crucial to have these conversations if you want the relationship to continue in healthy ways. Moving in different directions where one of the partners is unaware can cause significant conflict and will most likely blow up eventually.

Having a more open relationship where one or more partners form sexual or emotional connections with others does not necessarily diminish the validity of the connection or cause internal problems that hurl the people toward breaking up quicker than monogamous ones. Having this type of relationship does come with some very unique challenges. What constitutes physical or sexual cheating is a relatively straight-forward conversation to have. You just have to determine if it is acceptable or inappropriate to lick, fondle, screw, pound, or attack particular parts of other people's bodies.

Emotional cheating can prove to be one of the most viscous killers of any bond, regardless if pursuing an open or monogamous relationship. This can happen easily behind the back of a partner or in plain sight depending on how these feelings evolve. Many times, these types of emotional connections that tend to violate relationship rules can seem to come out of nowhere while other times they are calculated or come out of craving something that may be lacking in the current relationship. It's hard to tell if a friendship with someone is treading on dangerous ground unless each person is honest about their feelings and aware of what is going on internally regarding their emotions and attractions.

Regardless of what rules are created, the end goal needs to be focused on building a strong, secure, and fulfilling relationship for all people involved. Practice honesty, effective communication, and compassion when talking about these things. Relationships are much complicated and important than just what happens when getting naked. It is about building understanding, support and caring. Have these conversations to help ensure that your relationship is full of love, passion, and fulfillment without getting wrapped up in the cheating game.

Is monogamy important to me?

Most of us grow up with the idea that we should find that mate who makes us ultimately happy and pursue a relationship with them. In the hetero world, most people feel that monogamy is the only socially acceptable option for them. Of course there are those wild and crazy swingers and people in polyamorous relationships that break that mold, but they are definitely in the minority. I've talked to many heterosexual people about their envy of how gay men can hook up and have great sex with many people, even within a committed relationship. Many queers don't feel bound by social expectations of conventional dating, relationships, or sex.

There is a long-standing debate if gay men can be monogamous. I think that a more interesting and important inquiry would be to find out if anyone regardless of their sexual orientation can be monogamous and why they would want to be.

Many of us can agree to have whatever kind of relationship we want, including ones with tons of sex, no sex, vanilla sex, kinky sex, or "loud screaming wake up the neighbors in the middle of the night" sex. Of course it's normal to feel desires to be naked with a variety of people, know how they smell when they get musky from passionate sex, lick the crevices of their bodies, and know what sounds they make when they are in ecstasy. Desires and fantasies are normal, but living up to promises made in a relationship are extremely important.

Open relationships can be healthy or unhealthy for the people involved, but being monogamous does not ensure a higher rate of success or fulfillment. There are many ways to have a wonderful and hot non-monogamous relationship that provides opportunities for both partners to enjoy naked time with people other than their partner. Communication and honesty are crucial. If those qualities are lacking in your relationship, openness will bite you in the ass. You can set up whatever rules and boundaries you want. Some couples decide that the "don't ask, don't tell" policy that was so "effective" in our military will be beneficial to them in the relationship. Some get off on sharing the stories to turn the other one on or get ideas on new techniques and positions to be used later with their partner. Some want to see their partner enjoying gratification with someone else. You can play together with another person or couple. Maybe you limit sex with other people to playing together as a couple. This would allow for three-ways, orgies, sex parties, or trips to the bathhouse.

Maybe hooking up is only OK if you are out of town or with someone that is not in your circle of friends. You can also decide to set up a "date night" where both of you would be available to hook up with other people, socially or sexually. These rules can incorporate what activities are appropriate to do in these situations as well as setting limits on what not to do. Oral sex could only be allowed between the partners or condoms need to be used 100 percent of the time when playing around. Setting these expectations before actions happen can be a great way to reduce later arguments and hurt feelings.

If you are already in a monogamous relationship and want to add this element, figure out why first. If you're bored sexually or with other things in your relationship, you may want to work on those issues together first instead of trying to put a sexy Band-Aid on it by screwing other people. It may only serve to provide a temporary and potentially harmful pseudo fix to your relationship. Rarely can you fill a relationship void by getting your void filled by someone else.

There are definitely tons of reasons not to pursue a non-monogamous relationship. Many people may fantasize about having sex with someone outside of the relationship, but those fantasies can be crushed by fear that their partner will find someone hotter or more compatible. Maybe they are scared about finding a more exciting partner as well that would entice them to end the relationship. These types of fears can lead into behaviors like cheating or developing resentment toward each other or jealousy can start developing in the relationship.

Some people are concerned about the opinions and judgment from other people, regardless if they are friends, neighbors, or family. In all honesty, your relationship is strictly your business. For the most part, you can keep your relationship as public or private as you want. The key to any successful relationship is open and honest communication. Without this, things can fall apart. Topics may be really difficult to discuss, especially when your desires may cause your partner to become angry, think you're a freak, or bring up their insecurities. Open relationships are just a valid and have as much of a potential to work as monogamous relationships. There are infinite types of non-monogamous relationships out there. You could find one that works for you.

Don't yuck my yummy open relationship

Dear Brent,

I get a surprising amount of criticism about my open relationship. I have been with my partner for many years and the agreement about how we spend our time sexually with each other and other people works for us. Most of the time, these disapproving comments are unsolicited. When these comments are made, it makes me feel that there is a lot of unfounded and unwanted judgment put on me and my relationship. Why do people feel the need to tell me that I'm wrong?

Having an open relationship has as little potential negative impact on the quality of gay relationships as gay marriage would have on heterosexual ones. Much like opposition to queer marriage, there are those that have very strong opinions about what is right and wrong. Unfortunately some people choose to express beliefs to us where no reason exists to do so. At the end of the day, the importance of a relationship is that it is fulfilling the needs of the people involved in it. There is no single way to create a happy partnership with others and thankfully relationship dynamics are as unique as fingerprints.

How you spend your time alone, with your partner, or with other people should be an individual decision and based on what you feel supports your physical, emotional, and sexual well-being. Compare this to the variety of ways someone may enjoy a vacation. There are those people who enjoy going to remote places to unplug and relax on a beach, backpacking across a mountain pass, or laying in a hammock reading a book. Other people love being in the middle of huge festivals with sweaty men grinding each other while making out with over-grown muscle studs. No single option is better than the other, but it does matter who our companions are in these adventures.

There are fantastic open relationships as well as monogamous ones. Thankfully the quality and long-term success of relationships appears to be independent of their basic structure. It has more to do with the people involved and how well each person sticks to their agreed upon rules and deals with difficult situations. Partner selection and effective communication are ultimately the most important qualities in any relationship.

All that being said, I can feel some sympathy for some people who are searching for "the one" while swimming in the sea of people already in committed relationships who are looking for new friends, dates or to mess around without partnering up with a new person. For a single person searching for a monogamous relationship, those looking for an open relationship or already in one are probably quite frustrating. It is important for them to determine if they are upset with the individual in an open relationship or frustrated that they have been unsuccessful in finding someone for a relationship with them.

Just to clarify, sexual contact does not necessarily equal

love, but looking for sexual activities outside of a relationship or through casual contact does not necessarily mean that you aren't looking for a meaningful connection with someone. There are those out there that enjoy linking with people in a variety of ways. This can include sharing common interests, beliefs, great conversations, or mind-blowing orgasms. The only limitations we put on the composition of our relationships should be from us and our partners. One type of relationship is no more or less valid or beautiful than any other. Be careful about using your voice to pass judgment on other people or situations. Speak from the heart about what is right for us.

Is monogamy the new fringe sexual behavior?

I have so many conversations and emails about gay people not having the capacity to be monogamous, the majority of relationship being open, and the frustration that many people feel when searching for that elusive partner for a relationship. Some out there feel that all the "good ones" are already taken or the only people that hit on them are just looking for some extra-curricular fun without the hope or ability to commit further. At times it seems that those interested in monogamous relationships may be becoming more of a rarity in our community.

In some ways, coming out as desiring monogamy could feel a little like first coming out about your sexuality. You could get questions about what you think made you want to be monogamous or that the right opportunity could make you "switch teams" to pursue an open relationship. You may be told that it is most likely just a phase that you will outgrow or you will have a much more difficult time finding someone because of this choice. In these ways, monogamy could make you feel abnormal when compared to others around you. I know many people personally, professionally, and socially who report looking for that same mysterious "needle in a haystack guy" who is interested in a monogamous relationship. I wonder what is keeping them from meeting each other.

I'm not confident that successful monogamy doesn't exist in our culture or that it is really that rare. Historically, the gays have been perceived to be on the cutting edge of many forms of sexual expression. We have embraced kink, open relationships, and fought valiantly to be accepted on a variety of fronts. I think that it is amazing and beautiful to know that we have the potential for fantastic relationships and have the ability to form it in any way we see fit.

There are many reasons to pursue a monogamous relationship, but you have to be honest with yourself about what your personal reasons are. Some people truly feel that "wuv, twoo wuv" means never being sexual with anyone else. Others may believe that having an open relationship is a way to not have to deal with interpersonal issues and allow relationship concerns to be covered up and ignored by screwing other people. Some may be overwhelmed with feelings of jealousy of the thought or sight of seeing their partner being intimate with someone else or fearful that they will find someone more emotionally, socially, financially, sexually, or physically compatible. Of course there are people who feel that when they find that right person, intimacy with others is not desired and would be inappropriate.

In the grand scheme, monogamy is just one of the many things that couples have to agree on within a relationship. Take time and consider if you want a monogamous relationship in the beginning, but may be open to the idea of including others for naked fun at some point in the future. If that is absolutely a deal breaker for you in any way, make that known. That will help to form a statement about your desires for others to evaluate if that works for them. Finding compatible people for us to date can be frustrating for us. Figure out what we want in a partner so it can be communicated to others.

When using online and technology-based resources, keep

in mind that your profile is the best tool to educate people about what you want and tantalize them to want to chat with you. Be careful about coming across angry or bitter about your search for monogamy. Put out what you are ultimately looking for in a partner, but also be aware that meeting someone for a friendly hike or bite doesn't have to turn into a hot, sweaty romp or a committed relationship right away. Make your ultimate intentions known, but don't become so rigid that you may be passing up a fun time with a great person. Friendships can be developed where they may turn you onto a new restaurant, great workout routine, or a handsome buddy who may have the same monogamous-focused relationship desire that you do.

Is it time to end my relationship?

Dear Brent,

I've been in my relationship for more than nine years. When we got together we both fell deeply in love with each other and moved very quickly. Now all this time has passed and I'm not sure why we are still together. There is really nothing terribly wrong, but we have totally different interests and don't do many things together. I feel like he is more like a roommate than a partner. I care about him, but I'm definitely not in love with him. My biggest concern is that we have been together for so long and I'm scared about starting over. What should I do?

It is common for relationships to change over time. The best situations occur when couples change together in complimentary ways. Many of us have grown up with the idea that there is someone out there that is a perfect match for us, will complete us, and that is our soul mate forever and ever. Unfortunately those stories are most often works of fiction that don't translate well to the real world.

As we evolve as individuals throughout life, the core of who we are can remain the same, but our bodies, passions, and motivations definitely change. There are so many ways that couples can grow apart. They may find new things that interest them or become bored with falling into routines. Relationships have more of a chance of ending if they don't have the passion and positivity to counteract these changes.

I would suggest first looking at your relationship without your insecurity about your future. Figure out if this relationship is right for you. When we get into relationships, it is because we have found someone who enriches our life and we care about. This realization causes the exciting magic time when we decide that getting into a relationship with this person is a good idea. When relationships fail to be beneficial to us, it is time to determine why it isn't working, change it, or move onto another opportunity. Spend some time thinking about what is really wrong instead of simply chalking it up to moving in different directions from each other.

A lot of times when someone is violent, cheats, or abuses alcohol or drugs, it might be easier for a partner to decide that the relationship no longer is good for them. When situations are not so extremely negative, the decision may be much harder to make. If something really isn't terribly bad or good, the motivation to get away from it decreases. Many people make decisions in their lives focusing on the amount of fear and discomfort it will potentially cause for them. For those things that can cause a large amount of disruption in your life, it feels more important that you weigh out options more carefully. Making a wrong decision about where to have lunch provides much less of a life impact that deciding to quit your job and move to Hutchinson, Kansas.

Fear is one of the most ominous and stifling emotions. It can keep us safe when we are afraid of getting a speeding ticket or driving drunk. It can also stop us from doing things we want to do or seeing situations logically. When ending relationships, there is an innate fear of losing what you have, wondering if you will find something better, or wondering if you will never find love again. All of these fears are completely reasonable and tend to keep people in a very uncomfortable place until the decision is made to face the fear and do something different.

Talk to your partner. There is a good possibility that he has concerns as well. It is uncommon that one person in a relationship is in bliss while the other is in hell. To repair problems between people, it is extremely important for them to put the energy into fixing what is wrong or challenging. Sometimes we don't have the skills to effectively work through relationships issues. There are many tools and techniques from books written on the subject and professionals that are skilled in helping couples navigate rough waters.

At the end of the day, your decision may be to end the relationship and move on to the next chapter in your life. Staying in a long-term situation can be a beautiful accomplishment unless it is miserable to be in. Regardless of your outcome, hopefully you can both be mature and respectful. In these situations where emotions run hot, things can get out of control quickly. Take the effort to be thoughtful to each other through this process.

When to run away

As we have opportunities to meet a variety of people throughout our lives, we will hopefully find some of them intriguing enough to date. They can turn us on, share fun moments, become involved with our friends, and add to our overall enjoyment by giving us someone consistent to curl up with. Over time, we may also find that these people may not be the right choice for us. They may want to move in different directions or be a complete tragic basket case.

Often, the honeymoon period happens when it seems like you could talk or text all the time, never get enough of the other person, not have an argument, or think of a problem that could not be conquered by your love for each other.

Unfortunately reality sinks in and we realize that every relationship has its unique set of challenges and conflicts. The idea that we won't have issues in relationships is unrealistic, but there is a limit to how much we are willing to put up with before we want to pick up our toys and leave to find new playmates.

There are certain things like physical abuse or cheating that may make it easier for people to call it quits with someone. Other negative situations may be a little more difficult to determine if leaving is the best option. A partner's lack of motivation, drug use, bitchy attitudes, poor communication, or lame friends may cause us to question whether to end it or try to make it work. There are often times where our inner voice tells us that a situation is not good, but we may use our powers of justification to keep us from making the move that we feel is best. Hoping that someone will change often doesn't work and we are left feeling resentful and trapped. If individuals are not willing to make compromises in a relationship and work on those things that cause conflict, long-term potential won't be a reality.

On a darker side, there are also those people who lie to us and tell us what we want to hear to get what they want. As we come to realize that we may have been deceived, the person that we have fallen for becomes less of a reality and more of a detriment to our fulfillment. This dishonesty might get us to fall for them initially, but a false image can't be sustained for long and these people will eventually begin to show their true colors to us. This type of deception is sometimes a very conscious effort by them to fake us out, but there are also situations where we lie to ourselves because we really want to make a relationship work with someone and refuse to identify that there are very significant concerns that should be addressed. There will hopefully only be a limited amount of times we have to eat at a bad restaurant before deciding that there are probably better options out there to satisfy our hunger or would be more worth our hard earned money.

It is important to balance the need to work through issues in relationships with identifying when these issues are simply not worth the effort to resolve them. It may be difficult to know how much work needs to be put into a failing situation before you decide that your dedication to it is a failing venture. It can be difficult to admit that you invested a significant amount of time, money, and effort into making this relationship work, but it's not working.

It was a very wise man who brought up the point that it is important to know when to hold 'em, when to fold 'em, know when to walk away, and know when to run screaming like a little kid that just felt a huge spider crawling up his leg. For every day, week, or year you are in a relationship that is not healthy or gratifying, you are wasting potential opportunities for more fruitful endeavors. We are on this planet for a relatively short amount of time and I believe that we need to make every day count while working towards creating an amazing life.

Mom's advice for having a successful relationship

I got a stern phone call by my mom about another column I wrote about what moms might say about hooking up. She questioned me about why I didn't write about what moms would say about how to maintain a good relationship. The reality is that in earlier generations, many marriages were based around finding that life-long monogamous partner that you could celebrate decades together. We have entered an age where that is no longer the norm, but there are absolutely some very important life lessons that could benefit even the most forward-thinking, non-traditional homo. Even though our relationships may not last the rest of our lives or be with just one person at a time, here are some thoughts about how to make them as fulfilling, wonderful, and non-dramatic as possible.

If you make a mess, clean it up.

We all make mistakes. Perfection is a great goal, but rarely does anyone actually attain it. When challenging things happen or feelings are hurt, figure out ways to address the situation. Allowing these bad feelings to fester only serves to make them more difficult to deal with when you finally get around to handling them and can cause deep-rooted pain and resentment. Just suck it up because you're going to have to apologize anyway and attempt to fix it.

Think before you talk.

Lashing out when you're angry can cause even more hurt feelings. Off-the-cuff comments can come across as mean-spirited or insensitive. You may mean what you are about to say, but if it comes across in damaging ways, your argument isn't going to end well and the other person is most likely not going to hear the message you are trying to convey. You may also want to consider how your words could impact your partner or close friends. Compassionate phrasing is important. Discussing things that bring up issues like their insecurities may need to be handled gently.

Be kind to others.

At the end of the day, hopefully we all have a general respect for people in our lives. There are times in both shorter and long-term relationships where some of the sweetness and thoughtfulness may decrease over time, especially when getting into routines or when things get crazy busy. There is always time to say "please" and "thank you."

Honesty is the best policy.

I appreciate that some conversations with our loved ones can be difficult, uncomfortable, and potentially volatile. Being honest can be a huge challenge for people in relationships, either due to not wanting to hurt the other's feelings or because that honesty may make them look like an ass. Regardless of the reason, the longer the truth is kept secret, the more potentially destructive effects can happen when it is unveiled. Also, be careful about pushing feelings away to deal with them later or hope they will just go away. We all know what can happen when things are forced to live in a closet or pushed into a corner.

You can do anything you set your mind to.

This idea applies to a variety of life situations that can happen to us. It doesn't matter if you are trying to figure out a way to purchase a home, get in shape, finance a European vacation, or build up the courage to go out in those new sequined hot shorts. It is important to remember that there are times when life and particular situations can be more difficult than others, but there aren't many things that are so difficult or catastrophic that we can't figure out ways to make them work.

CHAPTER 7: SEX

Why are one-time hookups awesome?

Dear Brent,

Some feel that the guy who has sex with someone once then loses all interest and never calls you back is an asshole. Actually, I am that guy. I love sex, but to me, unzipping a guy's fly is like unwrapping a present. It's no fun if you've already seen what's in there. I'm not like that with every guy, but it happens a lot. I feel like a douchebag when someone wants to come over a second time and at most I just want to be friends. They say I'm "afraid of intimacy or "on a conquest," but I really think it's just how I'm wired. Is there an explanation for this or am I just this way?

You get off on the excitement of getting down and dirty with someone new. During that first encounter, you get to experience powerful sexual tension, strip off his clothes, kiss him deeply, taste his salty neck, feel him as he grinds into you, enjoy how he uses his mouth on parts of your body, feeling the muscles strain, and achieving a mind-blowing orgasm that covers both of you and splashes the headboard. I'm just taking a stab in the dark, but if it is anything like that, I think I may have some type of understanding about what you enjoy. Being sexual with someone can be an amazing experience.

All homo-erotic imagery and smartass comments aside, your interests and behaviors relating to the excitement of getting off with a new person are quite common. As far as I know, there are no concrete biological reasons for these specific desires. Of course that being said, humans are one of the very few species that shows patterns of getting off sexually simply for personal pleasure. Although there is no organic reason either for monogamy or wanting to screw a different football team every week, there are many things to consider about your patterns.

First of all, there is nothing innately wrong with getting sweaty and filthy with others, but we may value sexual contact for different reasons. We can do it to show affection to someone while other people attempt to increase their feelings of self-esteem and self-importance through the people they screw. Others try to gain acceptance, love, or a sense of purpose through their intimate encounters. Sometimes, being bored, lonely, depressed, or angry drives people to hook up. Some are thrilled about the hunt and conquest aspects. Of course, there are those of us that admit that we are just horny people.

There is something very understandable about enjoying someone that is new, exciting, and fun. When situations or people get repetitious, boring, or difficult, we may choose to leave the situation or just not want to get involved in the first place. To avoid these potential circumstances, some shy away from deeper connections and relationships. This can be dangerous for a few reasons. It reinforces an avoidance of anything uncomfortable or those things that could cause conflict, but it also can keep us from establishing more than surface-level intimacy with others.

It is important that you act within your sexual boundaries and protect yourself physically and emotionally. I do think it is crucial to be honest with yourself and your partners about your motivations, limits, intentions, and what really gets you going. Maybe you don't want to go back for repeat performances because it wasn't that good in the first place. Your time spent on the prowl to meet up with people does not necessarily mean that you are finding great quality sexual partners. Just because you can get off with someone doesn't mean that it was necessarily a positive experience that you want to do again. A consistent search for new people or sex can not only be very time-intensive, but may also become somewhat compulsive or showing of a potential addiction.

I'm definitely a strong proponent of sexual freedom and embracing those things that we want. I also believe that sex is amazing when people are truly connected and that it has the potential to improve over time when you learn how to make a dude's toes curl or discover his special spots that make him howl.

Balancing friendships and sex

Dear Brent,

I think that I'm a pretty normal guy who is chatting and meeting people in hopes of developing new friendships and trying to have some great sex along the way. I seem to be finding people either want anonymous sex or want to jump into a committed relationship right away. I'm not necessarily opposed to hooking up or finding a boyfriend, but neither is a really a big priority for me. I would rather meet good guys for hanging out and have sex with some of them. Why can't it be both friendship and sex?

It definitely can work that way and many of us have found those people who think similarly to you. I truly believe our culture is broken into many distinct tribes that have a variety of perspectives on many different topics. There are some that feel that sexual expression is something reserved for those whom you are dating or have a strong possibility of dating. There are others that are looking for a wham-bam, thank you Sir! Some enjoy interactions where they occur anonymously or with the "no strings attached" label where development of feelings is theoretically off the table, however sometimes they do.

Each of us has the freedom to associate with whatever tribe we feel most comfortable.

Amazingly enough there are a variety of other perspectives. There are groups of people that feel that friendship, emotional intimacy, and sexual expression can all be acceptable parts of developing interpersonal relationships with others. To some, these people are considered renegades, selfish or non-committal. It is somewhat disheartening to know that this type of negative commentary often comes from members of our own queer family that have also dealt with judgment throughout our lives.

Some people feel that sex without some kind of deeper connection is just an opportunity to shoot out a load. There have been many friendships that have been developed after a hot, sweaty romp, but that is because the people have discovered additional commonalities and the relationship has been cultivated over time.

I propose that these types of connections are just as valid as any other non-sexual ones. Getting naked with someone can provide amazing fulfillment and enjoyment in our lives while giving us opportunities to explore ourselves and others. I question those who are so pompous and overconfident in their ability to determine what is appropriate for the greater population. Just because it doesn't fall within someone's guidelines of what they are looking for in a relationship doesn't mean that it isn't a good thing for someone else.

Let's focus on how to connect with those people that share your physical, emotional, sexual, and interpersonal search for openness and variety. Being honest and communicating your desires about what type of connections you are looking for is at the core of finding potential partners. Although you may be more of a free-spirit, the majority of people out there may not fully relate to how you see the world.

Beware, there are some people that will tell you that they

are on the same page, but will secretly want to push you to change your mind and put the monogamy ring on your finger. Protect your own heart and sanity. None of us need more drama than naturally exists in our lives.

There are relationships that defy convention and challenge previous ideas of acceptability. Additionally, there are people that have a firm idea of how interpersonal relationships should play out. They may feel more comfortable in having some concrete expectations and descriptions of the nature of your relationship, almost like an emotional and behavioral contract. When all is said and done, it needs to be a good fit for both people. Compatibility has to exist on many levels.

I've been told that people with your desires are uncommon, but please have no fear. There are like-minded individuals out there for you to connect with on many different levels. I would encourage you to make efforts to ensure that you are being as upfront as possible about your interests, boundaries, and expectations. Continue your search and don't compromise your own desires and convictions to connect with people in ways that are meaningful to you.

Mom's advice for hooking up

I guess I'm a stereotypical gay guy in a few ways, including the fact that I love my mother very much and trust her wisdom on many topics.

For most of us, however, our mothers did not teach us the rules, regulations, expectations and methods regarding hooking up with guys for sexual encounters. Hopefully we were raised with a strong sense of what is right and wrong that can be utilized in these situations. It is confusing why it seem at times that so many gay men often take all those fantastic thoughtful life lessons, stomp on them, and proceed to do other things.

Many in our technology-rich culture forget the importance of being kind, respectful and having integrity. These people are the ones who don't follow through with plans, treat us badly and waste our time. Take a few minutes and think about what your mom would tell you about the importance of being a considerate and nice person when cruising. I don't care if your intention is to find partners for a walk around the park, dinner date, or an intense sweaty romp where you end up covered in spunk. Her advice would be the same about being nice to others.

Always say please and thank you.

This could include the usage of the phrases, "please show me your cock" or "thank you for taking it easy on my ass." You can also ask the person to please let you know in an appropriate amount of time if you are going to have to cancel a date due to unforeseen situations. Don't break a date because you have found someone that you consider better looking or can offer that special out-of-town-random-sex experience. You may also want to thank them for looking like their picture, being a great conversationalist, or making your eyes roll back into your head.

Say I'm sorry when you're wrong and mean it.

None of us enjoy being wrong, but we all mess up sometimes and hurt someone's feelings. It can be difficult to swallow our pride and just apologize. It's important to take some time and think about our role in causing a bad, awkward or frustrating situation. Taking accountability for when we screw up is also a strong sign of maturity.

Just because everyone else is doing it doesn't mean that you have to do it as well.

It doesn't matter if the perception is that everyone online sets up eight dates at once or can cancel one date if the next best thing happens to become available. Grow a set and be an honorable person. Many times the people that bitch about how lame the gay world can be are also the people that are playing games, cancelling plans, or disappearing after a really good chat. Be true to who you are and not engage in whatever game you think people often play. The people you will eventually meet up with will hopefully have integrity and honesty as well.

If you don't have anything nice to say, don't say anything.

I know it's easier to say than to do, but remember that being a catty queen makes you seem like a negative, grumpy person that will most likely talk a bunch of crap about all of your friends behind their backs. It doesn't help to build strong relationships in your life. Having a negative attitude tends to permeate many parts of your life and makes you unpleasant to be around. The other unfortunate aspect of acting in these ways happens when other negative people are attracted to you. They are no more pleasant to be around and can reinforce the belief that it is acceptable and normal to be mean-spirited, judgmental, or look for the dark side in everything.

Don't cry over spilled milk.

When something crappy happens to us, it's important to figure out ways to learn from the experience, move on, and try not to fall into the same circumstances again. Unfortunately, difficult situations and tragic people happen in our lives. Getting stuck in past bitterness about how unfair or unsavory it was only keeps us from living for today and setting ourselves up amazing things for the future.

<u>Is paying for sex wrong?</u>

Dear Brent,

There are times where I feel that paying an escort for sex is a real option for me. I get so tired of spending time and money on trying to connect with people for sex or a relationship. Most of the time, nothing good comes out of it and I think that it may just be a better use of my time and money to pay someone to satisfy me.

In my perspective, we all pay for sex in some form or another. There is a cost to almost everything we do. The phrase "there is no such thing as a free lunch" describes the truth that there is always be a price to pay. Going to the gym costs money, takes time out of our lives, and many times when we are doing it right, it really makes us sore. Getting a better job takes dedication, possibly more school, and maybe a little kissing up to our boss. Attempts to connect with people take time to chat, creativity to keep a conversation interesting, and emotional hurt when we feel angry or frustrated if things don't go well. Of course when things work out for us, we may be more inclined to think that the cost we put toward the venture paid off well.

In your situation, it's important to remember that there is always a cost associated with trying to make connections with people, regardless if it is for sex, friendship, or that search for that love of our lives. The costs of these activities could include much more than just the financial aspects of going to movies or grabbing a bite. It also takes time, energy and effort to work on connecting with people. Many devote time utilizing technology in their efforts to meet up with people. Hours can be spent cruising, many times leaving us feeling empty after a bad encounter, experiencing rejection, or just knowing that the search will pick back up soon after finishing with the latest encounter.

Your question is speaking to the price tag associated with meeting up with people. It definitely sounds like your attempts to connect with people in social, romantic, or sexual ways have caused a huge drain on you financially and emotionally. Take some time and think about your end goals for why you want to connect with people. In this search, it is important to know if it is only sex or if you're looking for a deeper connection. This can drive your actions and attitudes. If it's really just about getting off and you can afford it, get on the phone and reach out to a sexy rent-a-stud.

However, it seems like you are looking for more of a connection with someone you don't have to pay for by the hour who will actually enjoy your company.

Be careful that you don't give up on what you want just because there are challenges. Rome wasn't built in a day and neither will your social life. You may need to take some time and evaluate how and why you are doing certain things in the never-ending search to find whatever you want. Certain techniques are more effective than others and doing the same things over and over can cause frustration. It can leave you feeling defeated, lonely and miserable. You may need to switch up some methods and work on developing new skills or perspectives.

At this point, I'm not sure if you're actually considering hiring someone for sex or companionship, but there are tons of guys for hire and sites to help you find them. My primary concern would be for you to find your honest desire. If you're looking for a connection with someone that is based around true interest and deeper bonding, paying someone to fulfill that role will not give you that true connected gaze into your eyes past the time you can afford to pay him.

Hooking up with a cheater

Dear Brent,

A guy wants to hook up with me and I think the sex would be amazing. I know he has a boyfriend that he cheats on sometimes and hooking up isn't OK in their relationship. I told him that he should try to make his relationship "open" so he isn't cheating on his partner, but he is too nervous to bring it up. I keep on thinking that since he is already doing it with someone else, I wouldn't really be a home-wrecker if he gets caught. I think in this case it is his moral responsibility to be faithful to his partner, not mine. Do you think it would be wrong of me to hook up with this guy?

It sucks when your morals are in conflict with your penis. This type of war has been waged for centuries. I think you already know the answer in your own heart, but I'll offer some thoughts about it to help ensure you are looking at the situation from a few different angles and you will make the choice that is right for you.

There is a quote that states that "integrity is doing what is right, even when no one is looking." This really speaks to maintaining focus on your own set of beliefs and morality regardless what is going on around you. It can be challenging when something fun or sexy gets put in front of us.

Our mind is one of the most amazing tools for using logic and reasoning to solve problems or direct us toward a particular course of action. One problem with using your brain is that thoughts can be thrown into the mix that aren't necessarily logical, ethical or helpful. These can enter into our minds in an attempt to convince us that it is OK to jump in the car after consuming tons of beer since you only live a few miles away from a bar or to take a strange man's candy. Unfortunately when negative consequences happen after that decision, we wish we had made a different one.

Be careful about how you justify actions. There are always ways of trying to convince yourself that something is a good option. The perspective of thinking that something is OK because other people do it is definitely a questionable way of making decisions. Being a lemming can make you think that running off a cliff is a fantastic idea or wearing skinny jeans is awesome. Imagining incredible sex isn't the most logical justification for doing him either.

You may want to think about his questionable morality as well as your attempts to justify hooking up with him. No matter how you spin it, he is still cheating on a partner that is most likely unaware that he is out in the community pounding butt. By his own admission, his relationship rules do not include screwing other people and he is breaking a trust between himself and his partner. Sometimes our own desire to do things isn't enough of a good justification to go through with it. There are times when we need to look at the bigger picture and see people's creepy intentions or lack of honor. If people lie about one important part of their life, I wonder what else they may lie to you about.

Of course, we are all subject to free will, which includes your choice to hook up with this guy or not. Personally, I'm thinking that there are many people running around town that are sexy, engaging, and would be a great partner in some sweaty, sticky, wall-shaking, neighbor-annoying, dog-howling sex. These people may also be in a better position to be honest with you and others in their lives instead of sneaking around and being dishonest.

Most of us struggle when there is a conflict between an angel on one shoulder and a devil on the other. Angels keep us safe from harm, while devils can keep us excited about the more dangerous side of life. When our devious side crushes the parts of us that make us good people, we risk doing things that go against who we are internally. This can cause us to feel badly about ourselves or our choices. You are the one that has to look at yourself in the mirror daily. Make sure that you are doing things to support the best parts of who you are. Search your feelings. You know them to be true.

10 ways to destroy an intimate encounter

We have all been disappointed at times when we finally end up getting it on with someone. So many things could go wrong. Most times, people will not give honest feedback about what didn't work for them. They will often not interact with that person again and may divulge the tragic encounter to their friends. It is generally not good for anyone involved. Of course, this is only a partial list of things that can go wrong when being intimate with someone. Accidents happen like farting in bed, but most of the following concerns can be avoided. None of us want to be known as a bad lay.

Porn talk.

If you don't work for Titan or Hot House, then stop talking like you do. One of the biggest turnoffs is being told a line from a porno movie, especially if it is one that you have actually seen and recognize. Work on developing a better line than, "pound my hole with your big pole." Just use your own words or series of grunts to express how turned on you are.

Narcissism.

Mirrors in bedrooms can be a really hot accessory to watch each other get sweaty, but quit acting like Vanity Smurf and being so focused on watching yourself. Hopefully your partner will be worshipping your body so you don't have to do it yourself. If not, pick a partner that is more satisfying to you or go jerk off by yourself looking into a mirror.

Calling someone the wrong name.

So, it happens. Sometimes it is one of your ex-boyfriend's names you say in the heat of passion or maybe you are fantasizing about Ryan Reynolds while your guy is on top of you. Regardless, just apologize and move on. Hopefully it hasn't caused irreparable damage, but don't do it again.

Being rushed.

If you don't have enough time to fully get into the exchange and can't give it the respect it deserves, schedule another time with the person. It's hard to perform or fully enjoy the sweaty exchange when you are consistently looking over at the clock to make sure you are not going to be late or someone is scheduled to come home. Take the time to enjoy it.

No reciprocation.

Naked time is best enjoyed by the exchange of energy between people or a group of people. Hopefully everyone involved is leaving this interaction feeling fulfilled. It sucks when your partner is boring, lazy, or not focused on making sure you are feeling good. Dead fishes or self-centered partners make for a lousy lay.

Immediately running to wipe off or shower.

For heaven's sake, it's not battery acid. Just chill out and get cleaned up a little later. Cuddling at this point could be a good option or just rub the spunk into your chest. By the way, silicon lube is a great moisturizer for the skin if you already have it on you!

Too bossy or pushy.

There is a good possibility that this is not your first rodeo and you may not need to be instructed on what to do. There is a huge difference between telling someone what you like and telling them what to do. Offering pointers is often helpful to ensure that you both are enjoying the actions, but be careful about having excessive rigidity about how the interaction will go. Hopefully both of you are tuned into each other to figure out what feels good.

Stopping to answer the phone, text, or email.

Turn down the volume! Shut it off! Seriously, WTF?!?!?

No affection after getting off.

There are definitely times when we hook up and have somewhere to go or want your guy to leave so you can go to bed. Don't forget that we are all human and deserve compassion and respect. There are few things worse than getting a slap on the ass, a package of Pop-Tarts, and a few bus tokens after getting it on with someone and told to leave immediately.

Bad kissing.

There are so many incredibly wrong versions of kissing including "propeller tongue," "the slobbering dog," and "the pecking bird." For many of us, kissing is one of the most intimate things we can do with someone. Without great making out, going further might not be an option. Take opportunities to learn from some experts. Remember, practice makes perfect! In addition to bad technique, stinky breath is also another way to kill an encounter. Brush your teeth or grab a mint before making out.

Scared to come out as kinky

Dear Brent,

While I was watching our local gay pride parade, I saw a good friend walking with the leather group wearing a harness, combat boots, and a leather vest. Apparently we have more in common than I thought. Personally I don't think I could ever be that public with my enjoyment of dressing in leather and sometimes being tied up, but part of me wishes I had the balls to be that honest with people around me. I'm very comfortable with being gay, but I feel nervous that someone will find out about my kinkier side. Are there other people out there that share my apprehension?

For some people, admitting to an interest in kink can parallel experiences like coming out as gay, transgender or HIV-positive. All of these circumstances can cause some people to feel aspects of personal shame, fear, and embarrassment. There is a difference between being honest about who you are and divulging a blow-by-blow account of your encounters and conquests.

Kinky urges do not make you any less of a quality person or dictate your course of success in your life. There are doctors into fisting, lawyers into watersports, and truck drivers into wearing high heels or diapers. There is absolutely nothing innately wrong with any of these. Embracing and taking pride in them may be a different story.

There can be times when you are aware of these strong

internal urges and dread people finding out, being judgmental, and potentially exiting from your life. Although all these are possibilities, feeling dirty or ashamed of something may lead us to sneaking around and putting ourselves in dangerous situations physically or emotionally. This reinforces that what we are doing is not acceptable, shameful, and should be kept secret.

Your interest in kinky sex doesn't need to completely define you or permeate every facet of your life. You don't need to wear combat boots and a harness to the gym to show how hardcore you are. Not everyone needs to know what you are into. Personally, I don't know what most of my friend's bedrooms, playrooms, or bathhouse sex lives look like. Most of them don't blog about it, except an occasional dirty bit shared on Facebook or over coffee.

One thing to keep in mind is that there are some things you definitely can't take back once they have been put out into the universe. Be sure you are ready to own whatever you come out as enjoying. Embracing your kinky self doesn't have to involve taking out advertisement space. We all choose what parts of our lives we display and divulge publically. Don't waste time creating a new persona to unveil of your new and improved, kink-fortified version of yourself. There are huge differences between personal pride, being boastful, self-promotion and self-acceptance. Think about why it is important to you to let people know about this part of your life.

You also need to be aware of what information and impressions you are putting out publically online. In a world of instantly posted pictures on websites and streaming newsfeeds, you could become notorious in an instant. People can take screen shots of anything, post them anywhere, or email them to your mom or boss. This is not meant to make you feel paranoid, but awareness is important.

Remember that we don't live in the most sexually embracing or open society and there could be additional fallout besides people being judgmental and talking about you behind your back. Some people will see your interests as being concerning or immoral, but there are some that feel the same way about being gay. There have been some amazing people that have had their lives adversely affected by malicious people that are looking for reasons to spread their hatred, discredit them, or generally try to screw up their lives in order to gain some personal or professional advantage. These actions unfortunately can be brought up in court proceedings or job interviews.

Much like the process of coming out as gay, some people come out kinky quietly while others choose to scream at the top of their lungs running down the street in leather wrist and ankle restraints. At the end of day, what you do in your own bedroom or dungeon is your own business and does not need to be shared, analyzed, embraced, or judged by anyone else. The freedom to express ourselves in a variety of ways is an amazing gift that should be embraced and celebrated. There will always be people out there that don't get it. If they choose to express some negative opinion, just grab a roll of duct tape and a riding crop to show them the consequences of their actions.

Extreme sex needs extreme communication

There are so many forms of sexual contact out there and what is considered extreme to one person could be just a regular ride in a sling for others. There are so many sexual activities beyond having intercourse, including BDSM (bondage, dominance, sadism, masochism), flogging, water sports, piercing, breath control, role playing, or mummification just to name a few. These can be extremely hot for all parties involved, but safety should be the primary concern. Regardless if you are into kinky, rough or vanilla sex, positive communication is at the cornerstone of any great exchange.

Talk to your partner, partners, or favorite rugby team

about what gets you worked up and how you like to get to a mind-blowing place. Discuss your personal boundaries with using condoms, favorite lube, hot activities, and whatever else turns your crank. There is nothing wrong with talking about things before you start, checking in during the encounter, and after you're finished when covered in sweat or other fluids. Go back through what worked and could be different next time.

The internet has provided a wide source of information about many things including kink, but learning from written word, pictures, and illustrations may not be the best teacher. Before you tie someone up or filter electricity through them, do your research and talk to people who have practical experience doing these activities. Just because someone claims to be an expert doesn't mean that it's true. You can talk to others to get good references and feedback about some of these players. It takes more than the title of "Sir" or 'Master" and a snappy leather wardrobe to make them trustworthy. Beware of those who are boastful about their abilities or push you past your comfort zone. Take the time to find someone you trust and want to explore some things with.

There is a mantra when playing called "safe, sane, and consensual." This reminds all of us that activities need to have personal safety in mind. Don't come out of all this fun with unwanted physical or mental scares. Be careful about playing when the chemically altered, angry, or sketchy. Discuss any physical, emotional, or psychological concerns that should be considered before starting. Pushing personal limits can be fun, but ensure that consent has been given by you to go there. Sometimes these experiences can cause unforeseen emotional, psychological, or physical distress. Being with someone trustworthy can help ensure that your safety will be important to them and that in the event that something difficult happens, you can be taken care of.

Discuss what it looks and sounds like when you are both in ecstasy. Some like to use "safe words" that signify to your partner that play is getting too intense, uncomfortable, or needs to stop immediately. You can choose to use something out of normal conversation like "chocolate truffle" since screaming "stop" may be part of what is getting you off and you definitely don't want them to stop. Although using safe words is a good tool, it doesn't replace the importance of taking the time to get to know each other and each other's limits.

There are some that want to perform a scripted scene full of directed participant motivation, dialogue, and activities. There is absolutely nothing wrong with having a very specific kink or scene, but not everything necessarily has to be completely planned. There can be some kind of general discussions about your shared level of interest and intensity to provide some type of road map.

Take the time to get know and trust your partner while being careful about jumping into kinky situations with just anyone. Playing at this level can be a positive or negative physical, psychological, and emotional ride. Hopefully you feel comfortable enough with your partner to moan, scream, laugh or cry if these moods take over. Have a good idea if this is someone who will be there to take care of you if these activities bring up some strong emotions. These vulnerable places can be very terrifying if you are left to deal with it alone or with someone you don't like or trust.

One last safety issue would be about your physical health. Let your playmates know about any medical or physical concerns you have. Although kinky play doesn't necessarily involve screwing, keep in mind that there are many sexually transmitted infections that can be passed through sexual and casual contact. Before you get down and dirty, you may want to take some time to discuss aspects of sexual history, HIV status, and personal boundaries. These aren't conversations that should happen during or after a scene. Safe, sane, and consensual playing can be connected, hot, and intense. Don't get into a situation where you wish you had brought a ball gag because they are annoying or you want to beat their asses after a scene because they have hurt you.

CHAPTER 8: CHANGING PATTERNS

The insanity cycle

Dear Brent,

My life has never really been easy or happy, but in the past few years I've been even more aware that I don't like what is going on with me. I know that I should probably try something else to help me improve my happiness, but I don't even know why it's so hard to get out of my mindset and do different things. It seems like an easy decision to make, but really hard to start. Do you have any suggestions?

There are many of us that have heard the definition of insanity described as our decision to continue doing the same crap over and over while praying for a different result than we have gotten the first 4,612 times we have attempted to be successful at something. It truly doesn't matter if these attempts relate to trying to make a relationship work that parallels a Shakespearian tragedy or if we are consistently trying to repair our own diminished self-esteem issues by getting chemically smashed or overcompensating in a variety of ways.

Most of us probably wouldn't keep going back to the same restaurant where we got food poisoning, had awful service, or spit out the food because it tasted disgusting. Unfortunately, there are situations and people that somehow motivate us to keep going back for more disappointment, discomfort, or frustration. We may hope that it won't happen again despite our best logical reasoning that we should expect these repercussions and outcomes.

This may happen to us because anything we do over and over becomes a normal pattern for us. We can create habits that benefit and drive us toward achieving goals. Some of our other habits serve to impact our lives in potentially more negative ways. They can reinforce such ideas as helplessness, isolation and feeling like change isn't likely to occur. The longer we experience the same things, the less likely we may be to try to change them. We are all creatures of habit and it can take a significant amount of drive, focus, and energy to make positive life changes.

To get this ball of change rolling, take some time and figure out the aspects of your life you want to modify. These may be the ones that are causing you the most distress, but you may also want to consider those that you feel could improve your overall quality of life. Be careful about glamorizing certain changes by thinking that if you achieve these specific goals, your life will be so much more amazing than it is right now. Attaining something does not necessarily mean that your life will be full of glitter-covered unicorns. Very rarely does outside change cause amazing internal improvements, but they can help.

Be careful about waiting for the "perfect time" to start working on something. There will never be that single wonderful moment where the planets will align to quit smoking, start eating better, begin going to the gym, or start trying to be more socially outgoing. It is really easy to feel motivated to begin a diet after you have eaten an entire large pizza and are feeling regret or self-hatred, but harder to stay motivated and focused on pursuing this goal when you get hungry again or frustrated about something going on in your life. Great progress is made when the process starts and your will power keeps you focused, even when things get rough.

Fight through those times when you want to give up and don't throw in the towel.

Be careful of beating yourself up or feeling bummed out that you haven't been successful yet. You would think that feeling disappointed or depressed about something enough times would teach us that what we are doing may not be the best course of action, but it can take time to decide to modify our lives. It is important to remember that we all have the potential to transform almost anything in our lives. Changing long-established patterns can be challenging and uncomfortable at times. It can also lead into better life outcomes for us and aid in giving us the confidence in tackling difficult situations and gaining control over our choices.

Top 10 Bad Gay Habits

Much like the dreaded sandals-socks combination, there are patterns in our culture that make us cringe because they are so incredibly wrong. Not only can they cause high levels of frustration, but they also keep people from connecting with each other to build relationships. Some of these happen to us or we may be the perpetrators of them.

Needing to be discrete.

I understand that there are some situations like being Ricky Martin that could dictate wearing a fedora and sunglasses while an unmarked car drops him off in an alley while he meets a hot man for some sweaty fun to avoid the paparazzi. Most times needing to be "discrete" means he is already in a monogamous relationship, extremely closeted or super uncomfortable with his sexuality. Being stealthy and sneaky are not necessarily two of the qualities that you really want someone in your life to be skilled in exhibiting.

Endless messaging or planning.

Figure out if you have common interests, get some initial negotiation and planning out of the way, and then get together. If you're not really intending to meet up, quit wasting the time of those who truly want to form physical, emotional, or sexual connections. Also the questions, "What do you want to do to me?" and "What are you into?" can keep people on Fantasy Island instead of in each other's company. Be upfront about your desires and intentions to reduce the potential for people to become frustrated. Also, there are connections that can be best judged when physically in each other's space instead of talking about how it could possibly be.

Not respecting someone's boundaries.

Listen to what people say to you and what you read in their profiles. Quit wasting time and energy trying convince someone to step outside of their limits or proposition them for something that is clearly contrary to their intentions. Be careful about allowing your own desires to taint your impressions of what you think they may want. Sometimes emotions can shut our logical minds down and we begin to see things that maybe aren't reality.

Asking inappropriate questions.

There are a few that come to mind. I'm not sure when if ever it become customary to ask the size of someone's penis is or expect them to send naked or sexually explicit pictures of themselves. There are people who will do that, but don't be surprised when people are offended when asked. If you send these, don't be shocked if they circulate around your community and people whip out their phones to show pictures of you bent over a couch or smacking your junk against your hand.

Public airing of private drama.

We all have crap going on in our lives. Be careful about how much interpersonal turmoil, or "cyber-bitching," you do in front of others. Airing dirty laundry on Facebook or in the middle of the bar on a Saturday night can make you look pretty tragic. It is generally a good idea to stay away from people and situations like these. Of course, there are people who are drawn to drama like a moth to a flame. These people are generally not the ones you want as stable members of your social network.

Not bothering to show up or call to cancel plans.

Even if you are going to be five minutes late, pick up your phone and call or text to let your date know what is going on with you. Respect him enough to tell him that plans had to change and why it happened. By the way, the excuse that your mother's appendix burst only works once. Also, when you have made plans with someone, quit looking for something better to fill that time slot. Have the integrity to follow through with your promises.

Badly or inaccurately phrased questions about HIV.

When questions use phrases like "clean" or "DDF," short for drug and disease free, to describe their desired mate, it can send a discriminatory and uneducated message. More appropriately phrased questions could involve asking someone about their HIV status, when their last HIV test was, or if they use condoms, PrEP, or are taking their HIV medications regularly. You could also express that you are only interested in becoming intimate with an HIV-negative or HIV-positive individual. On the flip side, if you are feeling offended by someone's phrasing in their profile, you may want to express yourself in a non-aggressive way and attempt to educate them about less stigmatizing language that would get the same point across to others. Many times people will be more receptive if they are not being yelled at.

Refusing to acknowledge someone after meeting.

So maybe he chewed with his mouth open or farted during sex. It doesn't mean that you should act like he doesn't exist when you see him in public or online. Worse than that, maybe he is good enough for a 3 a.m. booty call, but not for a hug when you see each other in a restaurant. Treating people respectfully is not too much to ask.

Lying about relationship or HIV status.

Dishonesty is one of those human qualities that is born out of insecurity, self-importance, and a lack of respect for others. I can appreciate how difficult these conversations can be to have with someone and they may cause some form of rejection. Regardless, you may not get what you want at that moment, but at least your integrity will be maintained.

Arrogance.

We have all felt low self-esteem and awkwardness, especially from growing up queer. Even if we are not that uncomfortable kid anymore, got some counseling or have covered our pain with muscles and tattoos, don't think it is OK to treat others like shit. Remember back to when you weren't a popular guy. You gain more by being a thoughtful person than from being a cocky asshole.

__Gay liars__

Dear Brent,

Why are there so many liars in the gay community? There are times where someone seems really great, but after a while, they start showing all of these messed up behaviors and I find out that much of what they have told me isn't true or they are sneaking around behind my back. It makes me wonder if I am just blind or are they really good liars. Why is this so common in gay men?

It is funny to think that the general stereotype of individuals in the gay community is a person of beauty, compassion and intelligence who is financially and emotionally stable with strong morals and integrity. For many of us, we realize that this most assuredly is not always the case. In many ways, the gay community can demonstrate lots of external beauty, but inside there are personal aspects that can make us quite ugly as a group of people.

For some, growing up gay makes them really good at games of deceit. Depending on where and how we grew up, the world may not have been the most supportive place for us to come out. Many times we had to lie to our parents, peers, authority, past partners, or ourselves to be protected from real or imagined violence, judgment, or blows to our self-esteem. Hopefully we emerged from this personal turmoil being comfortable and proud of ourselves, but many times as we come out sexually, we can also come out being somewhat damaged from these experiences.

Many of us have taken the time and opportunities to work on healing our internal feelings of shame and weakness through our relationships with supportive friends or possibly a great counselor. Sometimes people feel that they need to create a persona or change how they present themselves to others in an effort to fit in or get what they want. There is also a phenomenon where people feel so insecure in their own lives that they try to counter it by making up lies or get off knowing they have influence over someone else's feelings and choices. This insecurity can lead someone into controlling and abusive behaviors including threats and violence, withholding love, causing embarrassing scenes, and being overly dramatic in a relationship.

One of the most public and sometimes private ways our insecurities can be expressed is in the use and abuse of alcohol, drugs, sex, and other behaviors that cause our relationships and lives to fall apart. When someone tries to counteract feelings of shame and insecurity through the use of these methods, they rarely emerge as a healthier person with stability in their lives. Most times, their surroundings need to completely fall apart before they search for help and make healthy changes. None of these negative behaviors improve a broken person's confidence, but can have a profoundly destructive impact on their friends and partner's self-esteem, emotional health, and feelings of stability. Many times these people pull down positive and supportive people around them.

Of course there are times when we are taken for a ride by a charismatic, quick-talking sociopath. It is important that we protect ourselves physically, emotionally, financially, sexually and spiritually. When pursuing any relationship, take the time to get to know each other, work on good communication between both of you and be honest. Don't fall blindly into the lovey-dovey honeymoon period where everything is perfect and you feel that you could never possibly disagree about anything. It is an unrealistic expectation and you will definitely be disappointed when it happens. Be true to yourself and with your partner about how you see challenges in your relationship and how they can be addressed. Regardless of their behaviors, at the very least you can be sure that you have your own integrity intact by standing up for yourself. Hopefully you will become more skilled at identifying these broken people quicker and with less pain experienced by you. Don't let these people keep you in fear of reaching out to find great connections. If you don't believe that being alone is better than being with someone unsupportive, then please take some time to figure out why you feel this way and hold out for a good choice. If you're lonely and desperate for love, you may not be in the right frame of mind to choose someone of quality.

The best way to protect yourself is to be aware of your own expectations, beliefs, values, and boundaries. Communicate them to your friend, trick, date, or partner as directly and honestly as possible and stick to your guns. Don't tell someone what you think they want to hear to get them into bed or a relationship. Understand that no connection will exist without some form of conflict, but also listen to your own protective inner voice that tells you to proceed with caution or run away. Life is also too short to waste your time "taking on a project" by working on changing someone or showing them a better life. People change because they want to, not because you want them to change. Instead of focusing on "fixing" these people, focus on "fixing" aspects of yourself that you feel keeps you from living the life you love living.

Subversive gay behaviors

At times, I think we all get used to the status quo and don't think about how certain attitudes and behaviors can affect us. There are times where I feel that I am surrounded by people spewing grumpy, judgmental, mean-spirited, and soul-sucking crap from their mouths and acting in ways that don't show that they are nice, thoughtful people. It can be exhausting for me to hear about and has the ability to impact my attempts to maintain a positive attitude sometimes. Let's play the "I spy with my little eye" game with these patterns too-often seen in our community. See how many of these you can identify in yourself or others around you.

Getting off is more important than friendship.

Sport sex definitely can be fun, but you may also have the potential to develop a friendship before or after you are covered in sticky mess. Many of us hunt for the ultimate sexual experience, but it can turn into a never-ending search that may leave us feeling unfulfilled and lonely at the end of the encounter. Friendships can be longer-lasting, more durable and offer opportunities for future naked and clothed activities.

Forgetting common courtesy.

If someone tells you hello in passing or online, you could return the greeting or do something to acknowledge them. There is very little energy expenditure on your part and you may actually meet an interesting person. It is surprising that some choose to be more impolite to people in their own communities than to a total stranger they pass on the street. Apparently not everyone's mother taught them the value of common courtesy or a simple "thank you."

Being psychic.

Be careful in thinking that people frequently fit some pre-conceived mold or you know how an interaction will unfold. You may think someone looks or will act like a douchebag or couldn't possibly engage you in meaningful conversation, but you can't be sure. Don't let your imagination stop you from a potentially great connection. Take the time to challenge your pre-conceived ideas about someone. You may actually be pleasantly surprised. Don't forget that we hate when people make unfounded judgments about us.

Putting others down.

This is usually done for their own benefit to soothe a fragile ego or poor self-esteem. These misguided attempts to gain some sense of power at the expense of others are an unfortunate waste of energy that could be spent on other fruitful activities like challenging themselves to improve their own lives. Being hateful does not support our development into kind, compassionate people or help us connect with nice people.

Thinking life is full of inevitable negative situations.

Nothing is written in stone and almost everything can be impacted by our efforts. Don't let the idea of fate dictate our choices. Take the time and energy into changing those things we want to be different. Be careful in thinking that you are stuck or trapped. Putting baby in a corner can really piss her off and cause a huge explosion when she decides to lash out.

Talking shit behind people's backs after being nice to their face.

I'm not one to gossip, so you didn't hear this from me. Okay, we can all be a little bitchy at times, but getting the reputation for being that person who is two-faced does not help to gain you the trust and friendship of anyone except those who are probably talking about you behind your back.

Laziness.

If you don't like a situation, your surroundings, or yourself, then do something to improve it. Stagnation only serves as a consistent reminder that you are stuck in a nasty place. Get off your booty and get moving toward something potentially better. You might not know the end destination or how things will turn out, but beginning the journey will get you there much faster than just thinking about it.

Inauthenticity.

It can be a struggle to figure out who you are and what you believe. It is equally as important to figure out what really gets you off, makes you feel fulfilled, and embrace internal qualities that make you unique and confident. It is more important to "be good" than to "look good." Stop worrying about what image you have to maintain to be accepted by other people. Work on liking and accepting yourself first then find people who enjoy those things about you. Being fake will gain you fake friends that don't really like you for who you are, but for the false image you project.

Being defined by tragedy.

Many of us have gone through difficult situations or times in our lives, but there are many that define themselves by their earlier trauma or crappy things happening to them currently. The clouds are always dark and brooding. Looking like a wounded bird, expressing self-loathing attitudes, or telling the same drama-filled story over and over to anyone who will listen only reinforces negativity in their lives and that they are a bummer to be around.

Not dealing with past issues.

Many of us spend our lives trying to heal the emotional pain experienced throughout our lives. Fear of rejection, abuse, and isolation can cause deep-rooted scars within us. No matter how much you build up your armor on the outside, if you don't strengthen what is inside, you are doomed to only be covering up a sad and insecure person. Take the opportunities to heal the illness instead of putting on Band-Aids to cover the wounds.

Are images deceiving?

Beginning at birth, we begin to categorize things and people. Some benefit and amuse us, while others really suck and can cause emotional distress. As we get older, our categories become more concrete and engrained. We also risk becoming more skilled at labeling and grouping people after an initial assessment. One of the biggest concerns in making these assumptions is that we can miss out on some amazing people because we feel that we already "know" them based on a few defining characteristics. These negative, judgmental observations keep us from interacting with people further because they have already been labeled by us as undesirable.

Many of us think that stereotypes exist as a great tool in protecting ourselves from harm, but they can also serve to keep us in damaging places when it relates to connecting with people. Spend some time thinking about what you have to gain by thinking badly about someone without knowing them. You may feel that it protects you from rejection and may be based on past negative experiences. It could be unfounded arrogance that you are better than someone or they may cause feelings of jealousy or inferiority to be brought up inside you. Consider what you feel about people within the following groups. Instead of judging a book by its cover, open some of these people up and begin reading their story before putting them in the bargain bin.

Muscle Heads

There are many reasons why someone would choose to take the time and effort to get in shape by picking up heavy things and putting them down repeatedly. Although there are some that do this to overcompensate for small junk or a lack of friendships growing up, some people honestly just like the look, feel and health benefits of being fit. Be careful in placing judgment on them by thinking they are self-absorbed cock-monkeys that are only interested in discussing workouts or becoming friends with those under ten percent body fat.

Twinks

Some people are just naturally smooth, have smaller body frames, and enjoy wearing T-shirts you might consider overpriced from Abercrombie & Fitch. These guys can do more than press their lips together and sneer at you from across a crowded bar. Be careful in thinking that everyone that fits this physical description won't be attracted to edgy, furry people. Similarly, be aware that everyone under age 25 doesn't necessarily place more importance on their hair and large sunglasses than their professional futures or self-improvement goals.

Super Successful

Be wary of confusing insecurity and overcompensation with enjoying nice things. There are people in our society that have gained success that supports a lifestyle where they can afford a fancy house, nice cars, and expensive clothes. Some of these people work very hard in their lives and are not necessarily spoiled trust fund babies. There are also people that work diligently to look like these people, so it may be hard to distinguish between the types. Be cautious of idolizing or condemning these people based on their acquisitions. Thou shalt not covet thy neighbor's Diesel jeans or judge them negatively for them.

Bears

Our world is full of a variety of body types and some are larger than others. In the case of thicker builds, it does not speak to someone's low self-esteem, laziness, or lack of pride in their personal appearance. Also, don't think you can simply entice them with a peanut butter and jelly sandwich with M&Ms and crushed up potato chips inside. Many big guys are just as well-rounded in their lives as they are in their tummies.

Body Modified

Piercings and tattoos have become commonplace in our society and it is becoming increasingly uncommon to find someone without at least one. If the metaphor of the body being a temple is continued to its logical conclusion, many of us chose to decorate it in ways that can differentiate us and make us feel more powerful in our methods of self-expression. Be careful in thinking that someone isn't kind, educated, or successful because you perceive their appearance as extreme.

Addicted to that rush

For many in our community, the use and abuse of alcohol and drugs has significant negative effects. It has the potential to destroy our relationships with others, but most importantly our relationship with ourselves. It can also cause a steep decline in the lives of those who care for those who are using. It tears our community apart from the inside out. In our lives, we should look for enjoyment and passion. When substances get involved, our lives can lose that pleasure and the desire gets transferred into trying to maintain the high.

There is a long-standing debate about addiction being perceived as a disease versus being simply a dependency on a substance or behavior. Regardless of your perception, unfortunately the "pill" prescribed to treat addiction can look extremely large and may need to be taken multiple times a day for a long time, perhaps for the rest of our lives. This metaphorical "pill" is composed of therapy, sticking to a healthy recovery plan, not giving into destructive desires, and reconstructing our lives. The most important aspect in this process is to maintain an immovable belief that addiction stops us from living the life we want to live and keeps us from the love we want and deserve in our lives. When taken correctly and consistently, this treatment can be quite effective, but be careful about skipping a dose.

Many times, people will not want to take this pill for various reasons. Some don't want to deal with the potentially adverse and painful side effects of not having this addiction in their bodies or lives. Working to stop drug use and other repetitious behaviors while taking this treatment will most likely cause some discomfort, either through withdrawal, losing party buddies, aspects of our lives seeming unfulfilling, or having to figure out how to live again without it. This is completely normal. People may decide to take it for a period of time and then stop for a while. Others will decide that it is not the right time to start taking the pill, but may do it later. Many are really frightened to start taking it.

For the addict, life is terrifying, reality is scary, and sobriety can be incredibly difficult. Many are promised a party when they start using, but the fun rarely lasts and the drug-induced celebration can turn extremely dangerous really quickly. Sobriety isn't always comfortable or fun, but having a life run by an addiction isn't enjoyable either. It inflicts pain on yourself and people who love you. A life without addiction can be incredible and fulfilling. It is possible to achieve peace back into our life. An addict can benefit by finding the internal desire and motivation that will drive them to face their demons, stop using, and recreate their lives.

For those who have loved people struggling with addiction, they know how an addict's actions can take over their lives in various ways. Supportive people can get pulled into a chaotic world where they may feel trapped and bound to actively participate in the struggle. As family and friends lose their ability to walk away and return back to their own lives, their reality can become entwined with the addict and they risk losing sight of their own goals, passions, and well-being. Until someone wants to change, nothing will change. Situations transform in our lives because we decide that there are aspects that we want to be better and we are going to take the initiative to improve on those. I know we sometimes feel that we can persuade people to do what we want them to do. Begging, bargaining with, beating down, or blasting on someone struggling with addiction will not only frustrate you, but will most likely be ineffective and may push them away from you.

There are many organizations that provide services for people struggling with addiction. Some offer support groups with others focus on cognitive or drug-assisted therapies. People don't have to go through this alone. Enjoyment of life can be found again. If this is something you want to change, do it. There is assistance out there to support and help you. This journey begins with the first step. There are many people along the path to help you regain the life you have lost.

Going beyond well-known addictions

Many of us have struggled with addictions to alcohol, drugs, tobacco, sex, eating, working out, or gambling. In addition to being drawn to substances or these behaviors, there are many social patterns, beliefs, and attitudes in our community that can also fall into this category. These potentially addictive actions should be monitored to assure that they aren't destroying parts of our life or causing pain for ourselves or those around us. Additionally, they can make us appear tragic and negatively impact our ability to create supportive relationships. For the purpose of discussing this idea, consider three of the more prevalent concerning behaviors in our culture: cattiness and bitchiness, self-loathing, and overachieving.

By definition, an addiction is nothing more than continued use of something or an action despite negative consequences in your life. For us, these outcomes may include having social difficulties like isolation, frustration, or a lack of healthy relationships. There can also be negative physical responses like limited restful sleep, nightmares, higher blood pressure and tension. Many times addictions creep up on us and we don't really think about how they affect our lives until they have already caused us harm.

Consider times when you tried to acknowledge when you are being generally bitchy and talking mad crap about people. Then think about how difficult it is to catch yourself doing it and then trying to stop doing it for an extended period of time. It is also extremely hard to challenge ideas that you are not good looking enough or too fat. Consider how difficult it can be to accept success when it has only been marginal or you feel that it should have done better. There are many things that are challenging to stop, even when we identify that they hurt us. It can be difficult to try to reduce the frequency some of those actions, but even more difficult to block the thoughts from entering our head in the first place. Over time, these thought patterns become more ingrained in us and may be harder to stop or change into something more beneficial.

Addictions are also characterized by having dependence on them and feeling that there is something important missing when they are not present. We may even begin to crave it intensely. Tolerance to the positive feelings of these may also be built up over time and we may feel the need to increase the frequency of them or the intensity of the expression to get the same results. Not only does this escalation not help us to solve whatever problem we are facing, many times our concerning behaviors and harmful thoughts intensify as well. Our self-deprecation and self-image gets worse or we become increasingly negative and judgmental. We can also suffer from never being pleased with accomplishments or feel that we will never be good enough. Withdrawals from these behaviors may be less dramatic than withdrawing from heroin, but can be quite uncomfortable in different ways and may make us feel strange since we may have been doing these for a very long time.

Don't get normal patterns confused with addictive ones. There are healthy expressions of these types of thoughts and actions just as there are more acceptable levels of engagement in cocktails or blackjack games. Sometimes it is perfectly appropriate to call out some douchebag after getting screwed over, have a low self-esteem moment after putting on a few pounds, or feel disappointed that you didn't win. It's usually when part of your personality becomes defined by these types of detrimental patterns that you need to be concerned. Unfortunately, many people struggling with addiction in a variety of forms are ashamed about it or don't see their patterns as harmful or disruptive. They even may not have the desire or ability to identify that they are acting in concerning ways that are quite obvious to everyone else close to them.

There are multiple ways to treat these addictions, but none of them can start without a firm dedication to want to change. Like with any goal, developing a plan to achieve it is going to be ultimately important. Do some introspection. List some of your most important and prominent qualities. If these include being grumpy, self-loathing, negative, bitchy, arrogant, insecure, self-involved, traumatic, or dramatic, you may be struggling with some addictive patterns. Sometimes these things creep into our minds and get firmly lodged in there. Pulling them out can be a long, painful, and frustrating process, but you can get in recovery from them and gain your sobriety from negative attitudes and harmful ways of thinking. Adopting new patterns and phasing out some old ones could cause a positive impact on your life.

CHAPTER 9: COMMUNITY

Finding where we belong

Throughout our lives, we may search for a group to join, a community of those who are like-minded, or a collection of people that share commonalities in hobbies, music, clothing, sex, or a variety of other activities or beliefs. These may be called by a variety of terms including sub-cultures, cliques, communities, clubs, circles, or organizations. Even as far as we have progressed though human evolution, there are still many ways we continue to act in tribal traditions by finding acceptance in communities that support and intrigue us. Inclusion in these groups can improve our quality of life, introduce us to some great people, and help to get us out of our homes to do something enjoyable, fulfilling, or community-impacting.

There are thousands of opportunities out there for our engagement, but only a limited amount of time and energy we can invest into these activities. The first step is to figure out what interests us and how we feel these groups could benefit us. After we figure out where we want to go, there are a variety of ways to gain membership. Sometimes it is more comfortable for us to be friends with someone who is already a part of the group before we show up for an event, but you can also choose to reach out to the current leadership or simply jump in by showing up and beginning to get involved.

There are many reasons to get invested in different groups or communities. For many of us, we enjoy being around great people and bonding with others. There are some around us that may seem to be social stud-puppies with tons of friends and a full social calendar.

On the other side, there are some that have been ostracized socially throughout their life and possibly have never been part of any "in crowd." For others, popularity may not have been a possibility and having a group that was accepting of them wasn't available. Inclusion and acceptance into a group can be extremely tantalizing for many people.

Regardless of our type of sordid social past, we can gain a variety of things from joining groups. For some people, the acceptance in these subcultures can act as their primary or secondary family. It could also make them feel that they are celebrated for who they are, what they believe, or what they do. Of course there are also people that simply want to enjoy their membership in a group to have that connection with others. There are others that strive to gain a leadership position or decide to take an active role in planning events and driving the future of an organization or group.

The acceptance in some communities may come at a price. Group members could dictate what is acceptable or unacceptable behaviors, ways of dressing, specific beliefs, or required activities. Members may not feel that they can fight against these rules passed own from the "group elders" that dictate how subjects in their kingdom need to act or appear. A potential member may be considered to not be wealthy or successful enough, too chubby, socially awkward, or inexperienced to be included or welcomed. Their rejection may be extremely direct or in more subtle ways if they don't fit the mold or conform to expectations. For those who have lower self-confidence or really want to join this group, they may be subject to feeling pressured to change themselves on the surface to feel accepted.

Sometimes it seems like our sub-cultures or cliques can also resemble street gangs in many ways. Technically, a gang is nothing more than a group of people formed for a particular purpose. These groups can also maintain a particular set of interests, values, and goals. Many times they have a specific turf that when interlopers enter, they can be made to feel threatened, scorned, out of place, or scared to be there. Breaking into these groups or trespassing on what they consider to be their territory can cause conflict. Whether you feel an association with these or like an outsider that isn't invited into their circle, it is important to identify when they serve to bring us together or break us further apart.

Regardless if you focus on beneficial or concerning aspects of joining a group, it is important to be aware of your motives to come into the fold and the extent that you will go to become a member. Hopefully you will find true friendships and enjoyment within it or decide to move on. There is also nothing wrong with creating your own social clique of like-minded great guys that maybe don't feel the need to join other established groups. Go get a bunch of people together and start having some fun.

Are we more than animals in a gay zoo?

Dear Brent,

I don't understand why guys in our community have a need to use terms like bear and otter to describe themselves or the guys they like. It seems so pointless and makes me feel like I'm trapped in a zoo. In addition to not feeling like I embody any of these predetermined types, I think it causes more separation between us in the community than it brings us together. Why do gay guys waste so much time on these animal names and creating separate groups?

I do find it amusing that our gay culture has moved into the animal world to find kinship, but I'm not sure that we are that much more different than any other group of people when it relates to forming sub-groups within a larger community. We have created some type of queer Noah's Ark with bears, pigs, otters, puppies, wolves, and other assorted creatures. Some of these animal-associated types may be based on how we look while others are based on activities that we enjoy.

In our lives, it's normal to look for those individuals and groups that make us feel welcomed and appreciated. We break off into clusters of people based on a variety of shared characteristics and interests including sexuality, religion, interests, and body types. It's also normal to hang out with those people who are considered attractive to us in various ways. These types of tribal divisions have been around since the dawn of humans on Earth and have evolved in the gay community to include designations like these.

Some people feel drawn to particular groups of people or commonly-identified types. Many of us experience a strong desire to be accepted by other people and included in group activities. Especially for those who grew up feeling isolated and without a collection of good friends, inclusion in a group may feed our ego and increase the perception that we are valued by others. We need to be cautious about using these designations to discriminate against others or attempt to hurt their feelings. Sometimes associations with these identities are used to exclude others from activities or may be perceived as stigmatizing to the individual or group depending on what characteristics are being discussed.

One of the largest potential concerns with breaking into separate groups is the adoption of group expectations and what constitutes acceptable behaviors. In the animal world, this kind of pack mentality is crucial for survival, but in our world it can be concerning.

As much as these similarities can bring us together, they can also serve to cause segregation and discrimination within a group and around others in the surrounding community. The group may attempt to dictate how we act in public or what is acceptable to wear. These sub-groups can parallel a clique of mean girls quite easily if not kept in check. Members need to decide how much of a pre-fabricated image they need to conform to for acceptance. They can also choose to follow their own path, throw the rulebook out the window, and not be a cookie-cutter version of a stereotype. Sometimes being an individual without the safety net of a clique can be a more challenging process, but it can also provide more confidence that you created your own image and stood firm to your own set of expectations and beliefs.

Don't feel that we ever have to adopt any particular image or set of expectations, but if these designations thrill and excite you, embrace your animal image and bark, oink, or growl at every cute guy that passes by you. If none of the previously mentioned ones fit your physical or personality characteristics, feel free to create your own. A hyperactive smooth guy could be a described as a salamander or a furry sci-fi geek could be a Wookie, Ewok, or Tribble. Although we are more than simply animals in a big gay zoo, it can be a fun place to visit sometimes and check out the exhibits.

Why are guys the same everywhere I go?

Dear Brent,

Gay guys don't seem to be any different in any of the places I have lived in my adult life. Most of them are flakes when trying to meet up to do something or arrogant when you chat with them. I have moved to particular cities because I heard that the guys there aren't like guys in other big cities, but I'm feeling really disappointed because I think they are.

It sounds like you move to a new city looking for a kinder, gentler gay culture where people are engaging without pretense and always follow through with plans. This sounds like you are looking for a magical place were all men embrace each other in brotherhood while maintaining high levels of empathy, intelligence, and a healthy sex drive. Unfortunately as you approached this beautiful oasis, you found that it was just a cruel illusion and now you're extremely disappointed. I think I understand where you are coming from, but concerned that the main issue isn't with each city's gay scene, but potentially how you interface with gay people in general.

Generally, when the same outcomes occur over and over, you may want to evaluate what is going on instead of doing the same stuff repeatedly. If it didn't work the first 500 times you tried it, don't expect it to spontaneously begin working. Consider your actions when interacting within various gay communities or during social events. Look to identify common patterns in your own behaviors. I doubt that you are simply an innocent bystander that keeps getting knocked down through no fault of your own. There are situations that happen to us without provocation and then there are outcomes that happen as a result of our own actions. Take a moment and see where your responsibility lies during these failed interactions. Take some time and figure out where you can change your actions or tactics to possibly increase your chances of being more successful.

Regardless of some cultural or geographic variations within gay communities, I think there are more similarities than differences and there are definitely some patterns that appear quite common across many gay sub-groups. Independent of where you move or which social circles that you engage, the only constant aspect in these situations is you. If you are experiencing the same things regardless of where you are, you may want to look in a mirror. Many of us look for a change in environment to change the way we interact with others or how successful we will be. Usually when this type of external adjustment happens, we should not expect the same type of dramatic change within us or how we interact with others. Some wait to begin working on something like increased social skills or self-esteem until they make a huge life change. Anyone that knows about goal setting or procrastination can probably tell you that there is usually no time like the present to begin making changes. More importantly, time can be wasted on thinking about how things are going to be so much better somewhere else or sometime in the future. This wastes precious practice time when we could be trying out new skills and fine-tuning those that we want to continue building.

Every new experience allows us the opportunity to expand ourselves and change the way we interact with the world around us. Be careful in blaming outside situations for something that could be improved on by evolving internally. It can be difficult to look at ways we can improve, but through this process, we can develop an increased sense of pride and confidence. We can strengthen ourselves and not continue feeling like the powerless victim of our surroundings or the people around us.

Focusing on the negative

Our gay history is filled with many adversarial situations that have been best met by mobilizing our bodies, minds, and voices in protest. As true injustices have been a part of our culture, our brothers and sisters have unified to influence social change and have allowed us to continue moving forward in our efforts toward equality. These types of demonstrations were about strengthening our community, not just because a few people disagree with a philosophy, policy or business.

Unfortunately the world is not always a fair place and there is not complete equality. It is not difficult to walk around a city and identify all the faults and things that could be better. Opinions are also plentiful when it comes to others verbalizing their feelings about a variety of issues. Although some are valid, others simply appear to be mean-spirited and focused on firing people up to become angry and shake their fists. These are a far cry from the influential and important protests of the past and present.

I remember so many gay pride events where a group of people stood there with their signs letting me know I am living a sinful life and will burn in hell. Those people utilize their right to free speech, but I have always questioned their motives. I doubt that they really think the expression of their opinion is going to change my decision to make out with hot guys. Many times, these people gain some misguided internal power from feeling like they have some correct impression about a situation or are arrogant enough to think that their perception is the only correct one. They may also get off on feeling they have some influence on other people's feelings by causing drama to occur around them. These people may also not have logical reasons for getting involved in a conflict other than to create something for them to do and give them a reason to feel self-important.

Unfortunately, these people tend to attract others of like-minded negativity or those who are looking for some drama-of-the-moment to support. Some of these people aren't even out in the public or part of a community and lurk in the shadows ready to grab their signs of protest, cause a ruckus, and then retreat. Others seem to find injustice in many places or may just be looking for the next cause to jump on. Many of these people have extremely loud voices of distain and may become addicted to finding faults where ever they can. They could choose to spend their energies doing good things for people around them or develop ways to make their environment or communities stronger, but being antagonistic and angry appears to be more fulfilling for them.

The reasons why some choose to become like this can be varied. Many times these people do not have fulfillment in their own lives and combat this by causing misery to others around them. By making venomous comments, verbal or written threats, and mean-spirited accusations, they can inspire others to attack, reinforce the negativity within their own lives, and cause drama within communities. This overwhelming focus on negativity may be expressed in different ways and directed at various people. There are those who see a friend's new relationship as an opportunity to remind them that men are dogs, will probably never be faithful, and to enjoy the brief relationship as long as possible before it falls apart. These are also the people that will turn a great party full of fun people into an opportunity to complain about the quality of the food or be critical of the décor.

Be careful about having these types of people in our lives or turning into one of those mean girls that we all joke about in our social circles. There will always be things and people around us that we don't like. Hopefully those overly negative people who constantly complain are not kept in our lives, blocked on Facebook, walked away from when they engage us, or called "Pappa GrumpyPants" when they attempt to take up our valuable time with pointless bitching. There is also nothing wrong with standing up to those who attempt to influence how we spend our days and pull us into their sticky web of negativity. Tell them that you are choosing to enjoy your time in the sun to participate in all of the wonderful things around us instead focusing on angry storm clouds.

Bullied slowly transforming into bullies

I've noticed a strange phenomenon that exists in our queer culture, but it also appears in our larger society as well. We have a really high prevalence of bullies around us.

I'm not talking about the straight (or repressed homosexual) kids in school that push the awkward gay kid into lockers or scream out the word "faggot" down the hall. I'm speaking about those that may share a common thread of sexuality, but definitely not the same regard for other's feelings and are guilty of acting in aggressive ways to others in their attempts to beat them down.

Being a bully is using your energy and behaviors to be cruel, intimidating, or controlling to someone else, especially those who you perceive to be smaller or weaker people. Most of the times in adulthood, people do not resort to physical intimidation, but choose to use emotional or social terrorism to bully others. Some would consider it being "catty" or just something that gay people do which is a usual part of our daily activities. Some think that it is simply a fun activity, while others have been doing it for so long that it just comes as a natural reflex that they don't even think about. It just comes spewing from their mouths, covering unsuspecting people with their hatred.

For many of us, growing up gay caused internalized feelings of insecurity. It's not bad enough that most of us feel uncomfortable about being rejected for many things including our own sexuality, but there are also times when other kids can be cruel and we feel really threatened. Some people feel they can use some weird form of power to justify picking on the kid that doesn't quite fit in. As we get older, these oppressive behaviors should become less prevalent in our lives, but sometimes they don't. I find this "adult bullying" even more concerning because of how much publicity has been created around educating people about the concerns of bullying in the schools.

Just because you graduate from high school doesn't mean that you are immune from people tormenting or attacking you.

Attempts to oppress and intimidate others can take on many forms, but it is generally done with the purpose to make someone feel less powerful, controlled, or be put in their place. The direct route uses cutting words, mean comments, spreading rumors, taking trash, or social media slander. The more passive-aggressive version happens where a bitchy look up and down is followed by a sneer and then turning your back on someone. It can absolutely signal disapproval, but is more geared toward making someone feel like crap.

It is important to remember that many times bullying is a sign of insecurity or overcompensation for short-comings or feelings of shame within people. For some, they may feel like they have gained some strength and security in themselves after feeling like a wimp for many of their younger years. Maybe they have found supportive social cliques or developed a well-muscled body. Unfortunately, being humble, kind, and remembering what it felt like to be put in a corner, ignored, or discriminated against has now been forgotten. Their oppressed and abused inner child has now been covered by the image of an oppressive bully.

Fortunately, there are people that have transcended into self-confident, successful people without needing to diminish others in their lives. These people have taken the time and energy to work on those parts of themselves that caused their insecurity to form in the first place. Not only have they developed ways to address these, but they have also replaced them with more positive and healthy substitutions. Instead of working to bury the sad child inside, these people have nourished that child and supported the healing and maturing process within themselves.

Don't get me wrong. There are plenty of other non-queer bullies out there affecting our lives, including some mean-spirited religious and governmental ones. I feel that this is all the more reason to identify and stop it when bullying is happening in our own culture. As we continue to make significant strides toward equality, I think it's a shame that we continue a social civil war within our own community.

Do sub-cultures breed drama?

Most of us can consider ourselves part of at least one sub-culture, community, or clique. These may be based around social, political, sexual, charitable, or other shared interests. As many of these affiliations can be a positive and affirming part of our lives, there exists a potential dark side that can emerge from these memberships as well.

These groups can function as a way to strengthen friendships or help create a type of extended family while providing opportunities for social engagement, fun, support, love, sex, and connection. It is somewhat understandable why some people respond with such intensity when someone talks trash about a particular group or a member within it. It's like a non-member of your family calling your Uncle

Chuck a "fat-ass drunk" or making fun of your hyperactive nephew. If your chosen community is that close to your heart or imperative to the way you experience connectedness, it may explain why some feel the need to get extremely fanatical and lash out when they feel it is threatened.

There are also situations where the importance for inclusion in these groups is due to a lack of having other friends or a connection to a larger community. Affiliation in a community has the potential to take on huge significance in people's lives. It doesn't matter if you define yourself as a bear, kinkster, goth, hick, nerd, A-list, politico, dork, twink, or activist. Some people work extremely hard to become members of particular sub-cultures and it can become a substantial part of their self-image. In some ways, it becomes crucial in their life as a way to gain fulfillment from their existence.

One of the main negative outcomes that could happen by membership in these groups would be a natural movement towards establishing a pecking order or a way of identifying the "cool kids" within that community. Regardless if it is comprised of a big group of "social misfits," many people will fight to establish some type of importance, power, influence, or social standing within the group of people. Many times these sub-cultures have an identified or underlying pecking order that can identify elder statesmen or those who have higher standing. This may be due to many factors including time spent within the community, attractiveness, or ability to pull people together. As with many groups, there are those people who attempt to climb to the top of the social ladder. Being the "King of the Muscle Bears" can feed someone's fragile ego and give their life somewhat of a meaning, at least for a little while. It generally only affects their self-worth on a surface level and does little to create true self-esteem.

When something or someone threatens to hurt the community or their position within it, strong lashing out can happen against the source of the real or perceived threat in their attempt to stomp it out. There are times where some of these people may not have the social or interpersonal skills to effectively deal with conflict. Generally, this is where venomous comments are spilled and group member's insecurities and negative attitudes become quite evident. It may be shown verbally, non-verbally, or in written form either in public, behind people's backs, or online. These conflicts that happen between people inside and outside of these groups may escalate from trash talking to verbal or physical threats of violence. Regardless, this drama only serves to bring people down and generally makes the perpetrators appear to be aggressive, self-important, controlling, unfulfilled individuals.

Be careful to identify your main motives to become part of any group and then to be aware of your actions as you become more engrossed in its rules, expectations, patterns, and personalities. Just because you have found acceptance somewhere doesn't necessarily mean that it is beneficial to your feelings of fulfillment or your future existence.

Super villains to avoid or defeat

In a world plagued with social atrocities, these gay super villains attempt to destroy our happy way of life for their own selfish benefits. Their abilities may make them appear powerful, but their actions are quite vile. Unfortunately for us, they all share the powers of entitlement and self-importance which usually shields them from seeing all of their messed up qualities and how they affect other people. It's important to recognize these characters quickly and discover their associated kryptonite, which can render them powerless. Become your own super hero by learning how to take these villains down before they have the opportunity to cause negativity or destruction in your life.

Captain Critical

He infiltrates your parties to talk trash about the food or the people in attendance. If there is any event or situation, he could have done it better. He also uses his powers to provide judgmental commentary on those around him including what he feels is wrong with people and their lives.

Professor Perfection

He is one of the most attractive villains in town and appears to be living the perfect life, especially because he tells everyone how amazing he is. In reality, these powers of false image are most likely covering up some large insecurities and a need to overcompensate.

Dr. Drunkie

His powers of bad alcoholic breath and overpowering verbal attacks can bring you to your knees. He also has the power to stealthily consume your favorite liquor at your party behind your back. He may attempt to use his other powers to subdue you sexually, but strengthening these abilities is often done through being drunk which often renders his penis functionless.

Blinding Bandit

Using his powers of deception, he can put you under a spell that may compel you to want to give him money or emotional support. He will use you for all that he can gain and then act surprised when his powers to influence you diminish over time and he is rendered powerless. Unfortunately it is generally after a long period of successful hypnotism.

Mr. Immediate

This villain acknowledges you only when you can fulfill a need for him. It may be that he is horny or could benefit from your advice. Maybe he needs help moving his secret lair to a new undisclosed location or it may be 2 a.m. and he needs someone to fulfill his frisky needs after exhausting all of his other options.

The Shadow

He lurks in the dark corners waiting to make his move. The heavy breathing and piercing stare signals impending doom for his victims. This villain actually probably won't approach or attack you, but his super powers of making you feel uneasy is still kind of creepy.

The Scarlet Beyatch

His bitchy powers directed at us unfortunately have the ability to diminish our own super powers of self-esteem if we do not put up our defensives.

Super Sucker

Not only does this villain suck all the fun out of a room, but he also has the ability to drain the enjoyment out of people's lives. His evil powers are replenished by people allowing themselves to be bled dry emotionally or through listening to their long, drawn out winey stories.

Hasty Mate

He can go from a pleasant social exchange to getting on one knee with flowers, a ring, and smothering powers that can cause instant feelings of discomfort.

The Canceler

This villain makes fantastic sounding plans and then proceeds to cancel five minutes before he supposed to show up or just blow off his commitments completely. His powers are replenished by absorbing the emotional energy of others who are unfortunate enough to make plans with him.

Need for mentorship in our community

Many of us have been fortunate to have those in our lives

that have provided motivation, guidance, love, support, and maybe a kick in the ass when we need it. These people act as mentors and can help us develop into more well-adjusted, powerful, and fulfilled individuals. When these types of relationships aren't formed, people can be left to figure out some relatively large life situations on their own. Many times it can take much longer to learn how to navigate or people can experience a lot more frustration, bruises, and setbacks than may be necessary. In many ways, having these mentors is much like having a coach that can help us increase our chances of success in learning how to play this amazingly complicated game of life.

Historically, one of the main strengths within the gay leather and kinky communities was the utilization of these types of relationships. In some circumstances, people were trained and mentored in safety concerns, traditions, difficulties, and methods to experience some amazingly intense, mind-blowing sensations. It helped to increase the potential to build a strong set of skills and personal integrity while decreasing possibilities for people to get hurt or learn improper ways to do something. It seems like the gay community's use of these relationship opportunities has decreased in the past many years. The AIDS epidemic took many of these mentors away from us, causing a disastrous loss of their opportunity to pass on their insight and the potential for some amazing friendships.

As we continue to heal from this loss of our important history I feel we need to return to some basic mentorship in our lives. This can help to build more empowered and strong individuals within a community. It also serves to ensure that experiences and insights are passed down to help guide people in the right direction, convey stories, share experiences, and teach tips and tricks to those of us that could really benefit from them.

We have all relied on teachers to educate and help us throughout our lives. These mentors can help train others on the importance of achieving life balance, how to live well with HIV, or why it's important to not act like a jackass to others. Growing up, we may not have received the kinds of support, education, and encouragement that benefit us as gay men. So many people struggle with feelings of loneliness, low self-esteem, and feeling a lack of confidence in kicking ass in their own lives. We also probably didn't get a lot of parental support in coming out or how to date guys. Many struggle alone, but we don't have to face these issues without support. Having relationships that encourage our personal growth and are there for us as we face life challenges is important.

These relationships can be valuable for both people. This is a great opportunity for a mentor to share positive outcomes from struggles they have faced and look at how they are leading their lives currently. They may also benefit by taking some of their own feedback or taking a hard look at the choices they have made. Having mentorship in our lives can provide fulfillment for all people involved and can help us create a strong interpersonal bond while increasing positive impacts on our community.

Of course there are lessons that we just have to endure, including all of the discomfort and consequences that come along with experiencing them. Regardless how many times we are told not to touch the hot stove or stick our finger where it doesn't belong, there are absolutely situations where we need to get burned and won't listen. None of us experience the same exact pain, discomfort, or heart-break, but there are common experiences shared by many of us. We need to step outside of our narrow field of interest and talk to some people with different life experience.

Let's get back to creating a more integrated and unified gay community where we can learn from each other again.

Straight people should act more gay

With sensationalized gay-themed TV shows, music,

fashion, and movies, you would think that the straight world would be challenged and motivated to start working toward embracing some of the amazing strengths the gay community can offer. Fortunately for us, we can provide much more to the general population than just how to coordinate your outfits and tips on picking out the perfect curtains. Many of us have found happiness and enlightenment in embracing and enjoying our gay lives.

Many queer people struggle with their personal identity throughout their early years and live in fear of being rejected or hurt because of their attractions. This can be an extremely traumatic process to endure, but it can also provide us an amazing set of opportunities to look at ourselves in ways that most straight people don't have to undergo. Of course, some heterosexual people may struggle with other parts of themselves that can allow them to experience similar explorations of acceptance. Although there are so many fantastic opportunities for straight people to explore, I think there are three specific areas where adopting some historically gay behaviors and perspectives could potentially set them up to be more holistically healthy, honest and introspective.

First, many queer people work on creating a non-biological family based around finding people that accept and embrace them. This goes beyond developing a great group of friends or a strong support network. It speaks to our desire to create an emotional closeness with others that rival or surpass what we experience in our birth families. For those who were rejected and hurt by their biological families, our chosen families can serve to support us more in our times of need and can act as a replacement of what we have lost. They are also there to celebrate when amazing things happen in our lives. They can help to be our moral compass or offer wisdom, but also act as valuable sounding boards when we need loving feedback or a kick in the ass. The creation of this additional family can also be an amazing enhancement to an existing biological family. We can never have too much love and support in our lives.

Some in our community embrace openness to relationships that push beyond conventional monogamous ones. There are individuals that are definitely built for being in a relationship with a single person where intimacy only happens with that person, but there is absolutely nothing fundamentally wrong with spreading affection. There are couples that break out of this ideal and enjoy other possibilities. With great communication and a team of willing participants, gay people have taken more opportunities to embrace our physical, emotional, and spiritual desires in fulfilling parts of our internal yearnings that may have gone unsatisfied otherwise. Expressing and sharing these desires with your partner can be a much healthier choice than denying them or giving into these urges by sneaking around and cheating. Feeling forced into behaviors that go against your passions can definitely lead into a whole variety of destructive and hurtful actions.

In addition to breaking the confines of traditional relationships, we have made huge steps in owning our own sexuality, especially regarding some really exciting kinky stuff. The leather and fetish communities have been at the forefront for many years. For many outside our queer world, being gay is dominated by ideas of who we have sex with. Since our sexuality has already been put out publically, I think we have worked to embrace many of these differences and we began to show the world that we were proud of the sex we have and the people we choose to have it with. Some complain that our community is over-sexualized, but I am confident that it also brings us to a more empowered place where we can feel excited to enjoy intimacy. Most of us are not shameful of being seen out in leather. The larger concern for us is being shamed by important people in our lives. The majority of us realize that who we screw and how we do it does not necessarily have an impact on our ability to be stable, intelligent, and successful.

As individuals and as a community, we have put significant amounts of money, focus, and hard work into breaking ideas of stigma regarding being gay, kinky, HIV-positive, awkward, chubby, dissimilar or rejected, as well as many other realities that could serve to keep us down. We continue to strive to become even more powerful, successful, and enlightened as we gain acceptance from the rest of society. These accomplishments could not be realized without focusing on who we truly are and embracing it.

We have had to deal with feelings of shame and rejection, while developing the courage and strength to overcome these by becoming proud, honest, and powerful people. Our community has been working on coming out of the closet and gaining acceptance in various forms long before Stonewall. Now other communities can begin to benefit by following in our footsteps. The courage and introspection necessary to lead our lives with authenticity is important regardless of sexual orientation. Hopefully straight people can take some lessons from us and spend time figuring out that they are ready to begin coming out as well.

Queer your city

I love visiting San Francisco. I'm stimulated by the energy of the people and the city itself. I've woofed at hundreds of men, made out with many of them, and cultivated some amazing friendships. When I am there, I feel that I am surrounded by my tribe. The first time I left after an amazing trip, I had a breakdown at the airport. There were more emotional outbursts for the few weeks after returning to "normal" life. For a long while, I toyed around the idea of moving there or to another city that provided more of a central gay population with expanded social opportunities.

Regardless if it was the right decision or not, I decided that it was more important to stay in Colorado to continue my personal and professional life. Despite all of the fantastic people at home, I yearned for the no-holds-barred, down-and-dirty, no apologies gay life that I experienced throughout my visits to San Francisco. There were many times I felt the cliché statement about leaving my heart there after coming home. Instead of uprooting my life, I made a promise to myself and my local community that I would bring back a little of the Castro and sprinkle it generously where I could. I would try to be a more confident, comfortable, social, daring, powerful, out-and-proud gay man.

I could live my life in Colorado like I was in the most affirming and supportive city in the world.

To hear some people talk about their home gay communities, it sounds like they live in the center of the most oppressive area of the world where no positive gay life exists. In most cases, there are gay bars, restaurants, businesses, parties and organizations within their reach, but also an infinite amount of other non-gay-identified cultural and natural opportunities to enjoy. Communities have created pride celebrations to commemorate our journey, give us opportunities to come together and challenge us to continue expressing ourselves in whatever ways best suit us. Some larger, more established events continue to be strong, while some smaller communities have created emerging queer events full of local flair and colorful people. These celebrations are fantastic and don't need to be diminished by comparing them to places like San Francisco. They stand strong on their own. It is important for local people to go out and support these communities to celebrate their initiative to throw these events.

Sometimes our focus on negativity and what we don't have causes us to be blinded to all of the queer amazement and potential around us. Think of the ways that we are fortunate to have what we do. You don't have to be in the middle of a disco dance party or a leather street fair to get your gay on. Even if something isn't specifically gay, we have the opportunity to make it gayer. The energy and dynamics of the people around you can create a more festive situation.

If you really feel that your city isn't gay enough for you, do something to start impacting it in a positive way. Get off your ass and change it instead of complaining about it.

Hopefully we have had opportunities to travel to exotic queer lands full of handsome princes and muscled kings, but there are also so many things going on in our own kingdoms. Don't focus so much on the limitations and negative aspects of where we live instead of searching out those aspects that make it beautiful and enjoyable.

CHAPTER 10: OTHER THOUGHTS

What do you want?

In a world full of diversity, there are so many things that can turn us on. Just consider the variety of ways people can stimulate us. In our exhaustive search to find those who make our heart, brain, crotch, and soul jump up and down with excitement, we are challenged with finding that complicated combination of intellectual, emotional, social, physical, spiritual, and sexual compatibilities. This connection can also come down to shared interests and life experiences, how you view family, and the ways you enjoy throwing around your hard-earned cash.

All of these exciting successful blends of qualities are obviously quite different for each of us and may change throughout our lives. They may cause us to feel attractions to a variety of different types of people depending on which qualities they possess. Of course, most of us value certain assets over others in our relationships. For some, an amazingly muscled body is so much more important that their knowledge about world affairs. For others, the financial ability and interest in traveling to far-away exotic lands is more important than introspection about the nature of the universe or what happens in the afterlife. Identifying those types of priorities is a necessary process to ponder so we can articulate the importance of particular qualities to others in our lives, but more importantly to ourselves.

We can become drawn to people for friendship, entertainment, enlightenment, or mind-blowing sexual exchanges. Hopefully all of us can list our top 20 qualities that we look for in others. It doesn't matter if there are some specific superficial qualities paired with some deeper heart-felt ones. I think it is important to try to keep everything in balance. Out of this exhaustive list of things we want, it is important to differentiate between those things that we unconditionally require and those items that would be awesome to have, but not absolutely mandatory. These may vary depending on if you are looking to pursue a coffee date, roll in the hay, or potential committed relationship. There are also those absolute deal-breakers that exist that will immediately take someone out of the running for any of those activities.

Many times, we can't necessarily pinpoint all of the reasons why someone is fascinating or eye-catching to us. It may be a combination of things you notice consciously, paired with some impressions that may remind you of someone awesome you knew years ago. Your attraction could also include a strange unconscious internal drive that you can't explain or deny. This fascination with someone may or may not make complete sense to us, but sometimes it's not critical that you can find an absolute reason for something. There are times were if it feels good, just do it. Grab on and enjoy the ride.

Realize that images we create in our minds about the perfect person or situation do not always translate well into the real world. If our desires are overly rigid, we may risk losing the opportunity to welcome some fantastic individuals into our lives. There are times when people may not match the image of the perfect partner or date that exists in our fantasies, but they still are engaging, exciting, interesting, and a blast to be around. Be careful about passing up amazing people. They may not fit our envisioned dream mate, but they can still be quite wonderful. Sometimes people have the ability to surprise us when given a chance.

There is not absolute perfection within anyone, but there are great people out there. We may benefit by taking the opportunity to find a balance between what we think we know about what turns us on and allowing ourselves to enjoy people for whatever they have to offer. We can simply enjoy these exchanges instead of sitting there with our checklist marking off their qualities to see if they meet minimal expectations for a second date or to be eligible to be your next boyfriend. Also, don't forget that it's not always just about getting off or finding a husband. Enjoying friendships and getting to know people can be fantastic as well.

Friendship FauxPaus

These types of challenging realities can happen during the course of friendships and generally cause bad feelings and grumpy interactions. Be aware or you might lose a buddy!

Vampire friendships.

These types of relationships can make you feel like you have had the life force sucked out of you. Regardless if it's draining because of drama, financial, or emotional reasons, most of these types leave us feeling more empty than fulfilled by them. Many times when the food supply for these types of friendships is cut off, they move on to feast somewhere else.

Not bringing up concerns.

We can all have potential disagreements and conflicts with buddies. Keeping them inside can cause resentments to build and may erupt when arguments happen. Bringing up a laundry list of character defects, questionable decisions, and judgmental perceptions not only will immediately put someone on the defensive, but may also make them wonder about how long these feelings have been going on without discussing them.

Becomes unreachable when dating someone.

Although having a committed relationship can be a beautiful thing, it can also be quite frustrating for those friends that are left in the dust while you are dating someone new. Strangely enough, these friends may be called on when things get rough or when the relationship ends. When friendships aren't maintained, it may be hard to get sympathy from them about your difficulties when you decide to re-engage them after a communication hiatus.

Fair-weather friends.

These types of people come and go in your life, but generally show up randomly or when they need something from you. Rarely are they interested in being consistently supportive to you. True friends are people you can count on to be there for you in good and difficult times. People who rarely are available when you really need them aren't friends. Be careful in putting descriptions on relationships that do not live up to the set of responsibilities that the title holds.

Social climbers.

Most of us work within various social networks, but some would consider these cliques. Some members of these groups may be perceived as having higher visibility, power, or status than others, while particular groups may seem more attractive to certain individuals for membership in them. Be careful of those people that will use others to gain entry into your group and then proceed to not live up to the expectations of being your friend. You can climb social ladders without stepping on the heads or hands of those around you.

Conditional friendships.

Unfortunately some friendships can remind us of high school. If you talk to certain people, wear particular clothes, or do not conform to super-important behaviors, you may risk being ousted from the group. Hopefully we have found unconditionally accepting friends to enrich our lives.

Not contacting unless something is needed.

It's great that people want help moving or consultation on a big project, but if you haven't been a good friend otherwise, you may want to reconsider your history of engagement with someone before asking for significant amounts of time, energy, or effort. Some ass-kissery, bribery, or promises to be a more interactive friend could be offered before this grand request is made.

Pulling into drama.

There are times where we may ask friends for opinions, perspectives, or advice, but there are also those people that can pull you into their dramatic retelling of a personal Shakespearian-style tragedy. Be cautious of getting pulled into their situations. You can become a key player unknowingly.

Friendships of convenience.

As long as you are one of the most attractive, successful, connected, or engaging participants at an event, these people may talk to you. Maybe they call you because it's 1:47 a.m. and they want some snuggling, but their other top choices have already found someone else. Hopefully your friendships are based on more than just because there is no one better around.

Talking crap behind someone's back.

In my mind, there are not many worse things than being inauthentic, especially when it comes in the form of bitching behind people's backs. Although it can be uncomfortable to confront someone or let them know that you disapprove of something they have done, grow a pair and use your energy to talk to them instead of talking to other people about them.

Your opinion of me is none of my business

We all worry about what other people think of us sometimes. For some, it inspires us to get up every day and put on a snappy outfit and look fabulous. For others, it motivates us to do a great job at work or be an amazingly attentive friend. There are also people whose decisions are significantly driven by the influence of others around them. These people may be preoccupied with how their actions may be perceived and judged by others or focus on doing things that are considered acceptable by the rules of their chosen group. In these situations, their own true personal desire to do something takes a back seat to what they feel others are influencing them to do.

It's not unusual that most of us have perspectives and opinions about almost everything and everyone. Some are verbalized, while others rest deeply in our minds and aren't shared with the outside world. Of course, there are those times where trash talk happens and some of these get voiced, many times behind our backs. It especially hurts when we become aware that someone doesn't like us or is critical of how we look or something we do, believe, say, or wear.

Of course it hurts our feelings and pisses us off since we are human. However, it is important to stop and consider a few things. Think about how this knowledge makes you feel. It's important to consider how these types of opinions from others can and will impact our life. Ask yourself: Why am I experiencing these feelings? Is this going to drive me to change something about myself? Does it truly matter what they think of me?

We can spend time, effort, and money trying to set ourselves up to be accepted or loved by those around us. When our own priorities shift to be more concerned about what others feel is a good decision for us, then we lose focus on making choices that are true to our hearts and our own desires become overshadowed by those from other people. There will always be social pressures and slick advertising that makes us feel compelled to want something. There are also times and situations where we may not know if we truly want what we think we want. It is concerning when our own true preferences and interests may be replaced with ones that feed into our strong desire to be accepted by others instead of taking the time and effort to figure out what actually interests us or turns us on.

Each of us only have a limited amount of time and energy in any given day to be used in completing tasks that can help set us up for a successful and fulfilling future. When energy is wasted more on what other people think about us and what they think we should be doing in our lives, we risk losing focus on those things that we really want to accomplish. Think about this when you have some quiet time to consider the person you are today and the person you want to be in the future.

Instead of our primary focus being accepted by others, I feel that it is more important that we work on seeing ourselves as a good person and to enjoy those things that make us feel awesome.

I'm not talking about building up our outside appearance to the rest of the world with an expensive car, over-grown biceps, or thousands of dollars spent on traveling to Puerto Vallarta. It is important to be honest with ourselves and those around us about our beliefs, passions, idiosyncrasies, interests, and quirks that make us wonderfully unique individuals. Hopefully Gandhi probably didn't worry about people making fun of his haircut or that Celine Dion wouldn't cancel a show after someone posted online about the size of her nose. Be careful about worrying about how others may perceive you and get real about who you are and the importance of how much you appreciate yourself.

Feeling the need to control

I used to get so frustrated when things didn't go my way,

which was most of the time. Even when I thought through a variety of ways my life could go, most times it didn't go as expected. I would like to think that I have control over many parts of my life, but apparently this is not the case. It was important for me to take the time to figure out what I actually had power over and which things I needed to work on accepting are out of my influence.

The concept of control is quite an interesting one to ponder. Many have sat under a tree wondering about what we truly have influence over, praying to a deity to provide something we want, or trying to build ourselves up with the assurance to go out and tackle situations. Considering that each scenario in our lives is comprised of about a zillion different variables, there really shouldn't be any doubt about why things rarely go how we envision them.

For many of us, there are frequent times when we may perceive life throwing us curve balls that we were not expecting. Situations, things, and people may also enter into our life that we did not see coming. Some of these are welcomed while others have the potential to cause high levels of disturbance. A few of these may be total shockers that turn out to be a lot of fun, while others may leave us scratching our head wondering what in the hell just happened. Fortunately or unfortunately, many times we do not have control over these types of invasions, but we do have more influence than we may think.

Life truly is full of surprises. The reality is that we can't always control when things pop into our lives, but we have the opportunity to decide whether to engage them, ignore them, or evaluate if there is a better time to pursue them later. There are things around us every day that could be beneficial or life-impacting in a variety of ways, but at times we may not see them. It is important to keep our senses aware so we can recognize when great opportunities are smacking us in the face. Most times, wonderful things do not simply fall into our laps. The skill of building awareness through opening ourselves to possibilities can be a long one to develop, especially for those who feel drawn to only identifying concrete situations that meet the image of success they have created in their own minds.

It's not unusual to experience outcomes that we did not fully foresee since there are very few of us that are as psychic as Miss Cleo. Rigid expectations are often met with catastrophic disappointment since most times nothing will ever live up to the fantasy we have created in our mind. Many people often struggle with the idea that the only way they can feel comfortable with particular situations is to control them. The idea that we fully have control over anything is unrealistic. This may cause our expectations to be a little out of whack. Additionally, our efforts to exhibit control in these situations will most likely only serve to make us frustrated.

I have found that relying on our insight, collaborations with others, positive communication, patience, and creativity can help us cope with life's unexpected moments. It can empower us to engage situations with confidence while helping us reduce our rigid need to know outcomes. Although situations may not work out to our full desires or expectations, they can still work out positively for us. Be careful about categorizing something as a "failure" that might really be a success or a lesson on how to improve future attempts. I think a great realist once said that if you don't have any expectations, then you won't be disappointed.

Common mistakes gay men make

It always surprises me how many patterns we see in our community that continue to impact us negatively. Regardless of what groups you hang out with, some of these continue to pop up. This list is most likely not going to be endorsed by David Letterman, but maybe Anderson Cooper will.

Big muscles and a handsome face makes up for being

stupid or rude.

I think the most important qualities for someone to possess are integrity, inner strength, and intelligence. Some people feel that muscles can compensate for many inner demons, but at the end of the day, these people remain insecure, sad, and lonely. Being an arrogant douche only serves to alienate you from people, except for those shallow enough to be impressed by your overcompensation.

Just because he cheated on his last four boyfriends doesn't mean that he will cheat on you.

It takes a lot of personal initiative to change any behavior. When a person feels entitled enough to cheat on their partner, it generally shows a deep-rooted belief that their desires are more important than anyone else's, including yours. Protect your heart and your genitals.

Some people are just naturally good at connecting with people.

There are only a few people that are naturally social studmuffins. Most of us have lived through awkward periods of our lives defined by not fitting into the popular crowd. Take the time to challenge yourself to break out of the perception that you can't talk to people. Put yourself in some social situations and try to strike up some casual conversations.

Going out or getting online is totally pointless.

Actually staying in your apartment wishing for Prince Charming to fondle you is totally pointless. Logging on or getting out sets your mind and body in motion to have the opportunity to meet someone. You can improve your communication skills, change your expectations, or hang out in different environments to increase your chances of meeting someone. There are a variety of tools at your disposal.

I will never find a good relationship.

This is one of the most destructive beliefs that can cause depression, isolation, bitchy attitudes, and a lack of initiative in getting out to meet people. Maybe a more accurate statement would be, "I am never going to marry Enrique Iglesias." You may need to re-examine what you are looking for and how you are going about finding it. There are many awesome people out there. Don't close yourself off to possibilities.

Gay men can't be trusted and are emotional train wrecks.

Many people feel that there is a high prevalence of dishonesty, substance abuse, and annoying personality quirks with people in our community. Thank goodness that this is not always the case. It is so important to really take the opportunity to get to know someone before you ask them to move in or make them your Power of Attorney. Unfortunately it may take longer than a few weeks to build that kind of rapport.

Being nice and thoughtful isn't valued in our community.

The idea that "nice guys finish last" isn't true, but there are some other things that can keep someone from winning the race. Be cautious about being too trusting early in a relationship or being too overbearing. Being caring or sympathetic is great, but it can be pushed to the extreme. Sending a sexy pair of underwear or buying two tickets to Palm Springs after your first date could be perceived as super needy and creepy.

Bars are the only places to meet gay people.

Many times these can have the highest concentration of gays, but we are everywhere. Start being creative. Go to coffee shops, parks, museums, social organizations, or book stores. Keep your eyes open for that cute guy that just smiled as he walked past you. Don't look away. Smile back!

Using chemicals to make you more socially comfortable increases your chances to score.

Careful! Being obnoxious, falling down, and making an ass of yourself is not a way to influence anyone to want to spend time with you. Actually most of the time people aren't impressed and your equipment won't work anyway if you do get the opportunity to get naked with someone. Keep your usage in check. There is a fine line between social lubricant and an oil spill.

That person that is too hot for me to talk to.

There is absolutely no one too hot for you to walk up and say, "hi." Being pleasant to someone after a greeting is hopefully a common courtesy. Be careful not to get confused about their intentions if someone returns the greeting. It might not mean that you should grab their crotch or that they want to sleep with you. Picking up on social cues and body language can help you figure out if you should continue trying to engage this person in conversation or move on to another stud.

Knock off the fake image

When we take a long hard look at ourselves in the mirror, there are a variety of people who can look back at us. It may be someone with confidence and a true love of their life or it could be a person who is unhappy with what is going on inside them or their physical appearance. Many of us are not thrilled with aspects of ourselves or our lives, but instead of working to address these issues, we expend an exorbitant amount of energy building up an image of confidence in our attempts to deal with these personal discomforts and perceived deficiencies.

Unfortunately, this new-and-improved creation does little to actually address the issues at hand.

As we become more reliant on these types of crutches to support our efforts to get out of bed, attack life, get laid, or pursue our dreams, the constructed image has the potential to overtake our true personality and become a necessary part of how we interact with the world. One of the most destructive parts of this faux-reality is that we do not take the time to heal the parts of ourselves that have led us to create this fake image. These continue to churn inside of us and bubble to the surface at some of the most inopportune times. As we are overrun with feelings of insecurity, self-loathing, and doubt, we may make the choice to do everything we can to push those feelings back deep down inside us because they hurt and we don't want others to see them. This discomfort and fear that these feelings will return to impact us in negative ways reinforces the importance of relying on this created image.

Throughout our lives, we are taught that hiding our feelings is a positive skill to learn. We can't always cry when we are hurt, cuss someone out when they deserve it, talk about feelings of invalidation at work, or admit to people around us that we are feeling weak or worthless. It is important to put on a brave face and get on with your day. Although this is an important skill to use at times, it also can be over utilized and leads us to an extremely unhealthy place. When the importance of feeding a fake image overtakes the importance of working through personal issues, we become liars and continue showing a person to the world that isn't real.

Be careful about creating "fabricated strengths." These happen when we work to generate an image that makes us look tougher than we really are. It may come in the form of big muscles, material possessions, or a seemingly impenetrable emotional exterior. For some it is preferable to look good than to actually be good. Logically, it is more important to have a strong shield than one that simply looks tough, but is actually made out of cardboard. Unfortunately some people have fabricated these types of flimsy images that are untrue, but appear amazing. These have the potential to disintegrate when exposed to particular elements in our environment. Many people get insanely defensive when situations are perceived to have a potential to destroy what they have put so much effort into creating. It threatens their security and is generally met with an equally intense emotional response which can include blinding rage or turning into a sobbing mess.

It's understandable why people work to develop these quicker fixes to their insecurities. In the past, we may have been made to feel hurt, scared, or powerless. Beyond obviously not liking to feel badly about ourselves, we also may have not had opportunities or mentors to support us in developing healthier ways of combatting the perceptions of our weaknesses. These feelings are quite real and have the potential to do much more than just hurt our feelings. They can permeate many aspects of our lives including causing difficulties in pursuing our passions, building close relationships, and propelling us to reach our potential. Although in many ways it is harder to heal those bruised parts of ourselves, in the long run it provides us the opportunity to become strong from the inside out instead of creating the illusion of being powerful.

Using a partner's psych medications for fun

Dear Brent,

I have an anxiety disorder and take medication only to take if I'm having a panic attack. My boyfriend doesn't have any mental problems but sometimes he likes to take my pills for fun. He's always asking me for some. Sometimes he even takes some without asking. He's not addicted or takes the whole bottle and I don't think using this medication is much worse than using marijuana or alcohol to chill out. I just hate how he treats my disorder like a fun chance to get high because I treat it very seriously, but I don't want to seem stingy or conservative. How should I handle the situation?

I'm glad that Lipitor and estrogen don't make people feel high or you might be dating a guy with low cholesterol and really large breasts. It sounds like you are struggling with feeling that your boyfriend is disrespecting the seriousness of your diagnosis and also you in general. It is unclear if you have tried to make him understand how it is affecting you emotionally. I'm hopeful that you have already expressed your feelings to him. If not, that would be a fantastic first step.

There are statistics that speculate that future generations' abuse of prescription drugs will overshadow all other forms of substance abuse. Although these generally are considered to be opium derivatives like pain killers and muscle relaxers, many of the medications prescribed to help with symptoms of anxiety or panic attacks are also easy to abuse. Depending on how he uses them, it could cause significant negative side effects to his body and, if combined with alcohol or other drugs, could cause some serious health consequences including death. I hope he realizes that there also could be legal consequences if he was to be caught using these medications prescribed to you.

More importantly for you than the physical and legal consequences for your partner would be how it makes you feel emotionally. It sounds like receiving treatment for this psychological issue is important for you. It also seems like your partner's utilization of your prescriptions as "party pills" is upsetting to you and puts stress on your relationship. All of these concerns have and continue to cause tension for you and could support destroying your relationship if not addressed. Also it is most likely causing more tension which causes an increase in anxiety for you.

In almost every relationship question that comes to me, I suggest analyzing how someone communicates their concern to their partner and how they can be sure it is understood. I am shocked by how many people avoid having a very frank and honest conversation with someone, especially when it could potentially blow up in their face or cause extreme conflict between people. Avoiding these types of confrontation only serves to help resentment and anger build inside. This can come out in a massive emotional or physical explosion or continue to be kept inside to gnaw away at their soul.

Consider if you are minimizing his behaviors to make them sound less severe and hurtful than they really are. You compare his behaviors to using marijuana or alcohol to relax, but his actions are also affecting the way you feel about him and your relationship. Be careful not to take these feelings you experience and shove them away so you can get over being upset. You might think it's easier to just "get over it" instead of confronting him and putting your foot down, but those feeling surface again and the resentment doesn't go away.

It also sounds like you are scared about being judged by him as a dull guy that doesn't appreciate the finer points of pharmacological partying or how to have fun. I'm curious if you feel that you need to allow him to continue these behaviors because you are concerned that he will ditch you or tell everyone that you are a buzz-kill. The longer you live in resentment of his actions or fear that he will judge your concerns, the more risk you have of hurting yourself emotionally and causing problems in the relationship. If you can't count on your partner to respect you, then prescription medication abuse isn't the worst of your problems.

Offensive things to say to a gay man

Although these phrases could be annoying if said to anyone, we queers can be exposed to them more frequently than the general population. There are many reasons why someone may utter these, ranging from being generally curious to being mean-spirited, bitchy, and judgmental. Be wary of those who may throw out these comments, but even more cautious if we are the ones slinging them. Consider if any of these comments or questions really need to be expressed.

You're a slut / whore / skank / dirty bird / big pickle diver.

I think the most appropriate response would be to simply say, "thank you" and move on. As long as all involved parties are informed and consent to said activities, getting naked and sweaty is fantastic. Throw on some gear and make out with 100 people. Go meet someone new that turns you on. Owning our sexuality can be a very powerful feeling. Keep in mind that the only way to get good at something is practice, practice, practice!

Don't tell my boyfriend / partner / girlfriend / wife.

Although some couples have a "don't ask, don't tell" policy for their extra-curricular activities, most of the time this statement signals an ethically precarious situation. Secrets can be concerning and cheaters never prosper. You also have to be careful for your own personal safety, especially if their partner finds out and comes after you with a large fry pan.

Open / kinky / polyamorous relationships never work.

Fortunately, there are endless relationship possibilities, activities, and configurations that have equal chances of being functional. This potential for success increases when the right people get together and have great communication with commonly agreed upon goals and expectations.

Who is the man / woman / pitcher / catcher in the relationship?

These antiquated labels still continue to pop up occasionally, but is more commonly asked through questioning if someone is a top or bottom. It's amazing that some people don't have the couth to not ask personal information, especially when it will not pertain to ever getting naked or having sex with them. I wonder if this information would be gained for personal satisfaction or if it needs to be disseminated to the general public.

You have really put on some weight / dropped some muscle / look rough.

Hopefully these comments aren't made to act like a catty bitch and hurt someone's feelings. Our bodies are in a consistent state of flux, but there can be dramatic physical changes depending on health concerns, life situations, and focus on one set of goals over others. Chances are that if you are seeing significant changes in someone's body, they are painfully aware of them as well. Better questions may be asked to find out how they are doing or if they need help or support.

How big is your dick?

I know this is a relatively normal online question and some people really don't mind being asked. Others take offence. Maybe if someone is looking for a huge piece of equipment, their request could be printed at the top of their profile or displayed proudly on a T-shirt. There is nothing wrong with admitting that you are a huge size queen.

Your relationship is never going to last.

Although they may be correct, I'm not sure why they would they feel the need to say this. This is usually intended to put a negative cloud over a relationship and give someone a sense of, "I told you so" if it doesn't work out.

Are you clean?

I love questions about the last time I showered or wiped my ass. Encourage others to research appropriate uses of the word "clean" in the English language and not use it in conjunction with sexual health queries. A more appropriate set of questions would most likely get to the root of your potential partner's sexual practices and health history.

Just this one time.

Some people try to push us into activities that could put us in danger or bring up feelings of regret later. This is why we have to know where our boundaries lie and be prepared to defend them. The regret and terror that can happen after we do things that may put our health or safety at risk can be avoided if we have the confidence to stand up for ourselves and tell people to bugger off when they push us past our comfort levels.

God hates fags. / You're going to hell.

This kind of hatred has hurt so many of us. It can have catastrophic impacts on self-esteem, suicide rates, people's actions to keep themselves safe, and the freedom to be who they are. Regardless if someone believes in an omnipotent being or feels that queer people are an abomination, there is no reason for them to spout off their beliefs. Tell them to wallow in their own pit of fire and brimstone because you have a fabulous life to live.

Recently diagnosed HIV+ and freaked out

Dear Brent,

A few weeks ago, I was diagnosed HIV-positive. It was a total shock. My doctor spent a lot of time discussing the science behind the virus, how the medications work, and that it isn't a big deal anymore since it is manageable and considered a chronic disease. I know I can live out a normal life with taking my medications, but inside I'm experiencing so many intense emotions, sometimes many of them all at once. I'm most concerned about how HIV will affect me socially, both with friends and family, but also with current and future sexual partners. Can you help me feel better about this?

I would love to tell you that having HIV isn't a big deal, but for many people it is a huge deal. There are tons of issues and concerns around disclosing your status to others, potential rejection because of it, and how to live your life after becoming aware of your status. There are most likely going to be times where your emotions are completely wacked out. There is nothing unusual about these feelings and the more you try to push them down, the longer it will take to deal with them. Don't waste energy fighting them off. It can take time and support from some wonderful people in your life, but the more actively you deal with how you feel, the better off you will be in the long run.

I'm not confident that there is a single perfect way or time frame to tell someone that you are HIV-positive, but I do feel that people absolutely need support throughout the process of coming to grips with the diagnosis. Don't feel pressured to come screaming out of the closet about your HIV status, but figure out key important people in your life that can offer you love, support, knowledge, direction, feedback, a hot meal, or a huge hug. Having a core group of amazing people can be your most significant support.

Being completely honest about your status with everyone isn't necessary and could cause some negative repercussions. Don't worry about telling your grandmother in a nursing home unless it is extremely important for you to tell her. Take the time to figure out how you feel before disclosing it to everyone in your life.

Although it can be uncomfortable to discuss your HIV status generally, bringing it up with a sexual partner can be even more terrifying. Many times fear of rejection and judgment causes tons of anxiety. Regardless of potential hurt, I feel that it is important for both parties to discuss what they are going to do to each other in an intimate moment and what levels of risk each of you is willing to take regardless of your HIV status. Unfortunately, there also those who feel that being dishonest about their status saves them from being turned down and will tell people directly that they are HIV-negative. Lying about this only serves to keep you in a place of shame about your diagnosis and is unfair to your naked partner. It is the responsibility of all people involved to discuss their limits, but taking the opportunity to disclose your status in an honest and open way shows respect for your partner as well as yourself. There is a certain amount of power that you can develop by accepting that you have a virus that has impacted your life and you are choosing to live a life of strength and integrity regardless of it.

Some people choose to lie about their status or not disclose it until later in a relationship after some trust and attraction have been developed. Others feel that it is better to get it out in the open before time and energy are spent on attempting to develop a relationship that would be immediately ended due to a lack of comfort in being with an HIV-positive person.

Being rejected by someone can be difficult regardless of the reason.

Hopefully rejection is given in a kind way without anger or hurtful words. This is not always the case. There will be times where the painful sting of bitter rejection may bite you in the ass, but lick your wounds and move on. It does not speak to you being a bad person, but only to their lack of comfort in being with someone who is HIV-positive. This may be due to a lack of knowledge about the virus, concerning experiences in their past, or a strong internal fear of becoming HIV-positive. Although you can spend time and energy discussing their concerns and educating them, it may just not be the right time for them to face this situation. I know it may be extremely difficult, but try not to take it personally. There are many others who will accept you regardless of your HIV status.

Whether you are HIV negative or positive, there is nothing wrong with living in concern about HIV and the effect it has on the human body. Surprisingly, some people continue to live in some form of ignorance about general HIV knowledge including risk factors regarding transmission of the virus and effective ways to reduce the risk of this occurring. Condoms have kept so many people HIV-negative throughout the years, but there are additional emerging medical findings that have a gigantic impact on keeping HIV-positive people healthy and HIV-negative people from getting infected. HIV treatment medications when taken correctly and consistently keep the virus level down in the body. When these levels are at an "undetectable" level when tested in the blood, the risk of transmission is extremely low. The latest research directly effecting HIV-negative people is the approval of Truvada as a "pre-exposure prophylaxis." When this HIV medication is taken as prescribed, it has been shown to block the HIV virus' ability to attach to healthy cells so it can't replicate in the body, allowing you to fight off limited amounts of HIV if exposed. Through these and other risk-reduction techniques, risk of transmission decreases and people can work on enjoying sexual contact without living in terror. It is every sexually-active person's responsibility to gain knowledge about how to maintain their health and act according to their personal limits. Unfortunately ignorance, judgment, and hate have the ability to hurt us both physically and emotionally. Fight both of these off by gaining knowledge.

This is a time of a lot of change for you. Even though this can be difficult emotionally, it is also important to learn as much as possible about HIV treatment options, transmission methods, and ways to keep yourself as healthy for as long as possible. As others have said, HIV is a life-changer, not a life-ender. Although this is something that you will need to live with until they find a cure, your life can be full of enjoyment, passion, new experiences, personal expansion, and love. Don't let a virus define you or dictate your life direction.

Using new, more accurate acronyms

There are varieties of acronyms and other terms that are used online, in print, and verbally in our society to describe people or situations. Unfortunately, many of those describing HIV, sex, and hooking up can be seen as discriminatory and mean-spirited.

Take for example the acronym "DDF," which stands for

"drug and disease free." It generally speaks to wanting to engage with someone who is HIV-negative and not using drugs. This term does not usually describe non-sexually related diseases like cancer or diabetes, nor does it address someone's usage of alcohol, caffeine, or nicotine. It talks about not being interested in people who use illegal drugs, which may or may not include pot, and those who are HIV-positive. It also doesn't necessarily address if people may have been exposed to other sexually transmitted infections such as syphilis or gonorrhea.

I am concerned with using these types of categorical ways of describing people for a few reasons. First of all, they are largely inaccurate. If you don't want to hang with someone who uses illegal drugs, simply state that desire. If you are looking to get with someone who is HIV-negative, then state it in a non-aggressive way. Be aware that just because someone tells you that they are negative doesn't mean that they are being honest about their status or they may be unaware that they are HIV-positive. My second concern with using terminology like this is that it can cause others feelings of isolation, stigmatization, or anger for people that would read your statement, even if that wasn't your intent.

I am putting out a worldwide challenge. Feel free to use the acronyms below or develop your own that can be used to describe you or what you are looking for in others. Start the revolution of empowering each other through words instead of separating and hurting each other by inaccurate or mean-spirited statements.

PUSHY – Positive Undetectable Sexy Healthy and Yummy

Here is a new acronym that could describe someone who is HIV-positive, but consistently takes their medications, follows up with medical appointments, has a low level of HIV in their blood, a strong immune system, and is at a hugely reduced risk of transmitting it to an HIV-negative partner. Of course, being totally woofy is an added bonus.

NEAR – Negative Educated Affirming Responsible

Here is one for a person that may be HIV-negative, but understands how HIV is transmitted and ways to reduce their risk of becoming HIV-positive. These people have thought through their personal limits and realize that there are ways to protect themselves without being afraid of HIV-positive people or discriminating against them. They don't let a virus dictate who they love or want to screw.

PONG – Powerful Optimistic No Games

This describes an individual that has integrity and an optimistic attitude toward meeting up with people to build great relationships. When they express interest or make plans, they mean it and can be counted on to follow through.

FLUID – Fun Lacking Using Illegal Drugs

These people may be sober, living in recovery, or simply wanting to stay away from people that use drugs. Additionally, they may want to express a desire to stay away from socializing in bars or clubs because hanging out in quieter environments can mean more intimate conversations and activities.

WHIP – Wanting Hotness In Person

Use this when you want to reinforce that being online or endless chatting is not as fulfilling as meeting in person. Get out there and go do something after an initial connection using technology! There is much more excitement that can happen when you are face-to-face.

BAD FEAR – Bullshit And Drama Free Enjoying Authentic Relationships

It would be so nice to find, especially when we really want to get to know someone. Hopefully this is what we are all endeavoring to have in our lives. It is important to discover early when knowing someone if they have the same desire for this as you do.

Live each day like it was your last

One weekend I got to hang out briefly with a fun guy while I was out with friends. We had spent some good quality time together previously and I really enjoyed our conversations and his energy. We made plans to grab brunch soon with friends when our schedules were less busy.

Five days later, I found out on Facebook that he had died from complications from cardiac arrest.

I was definitely saddened about his passing, but it made me painfully aware that we weren't going to have an opportunity to grab a bite, have a beer, or see our buddy's band play again. It's amazing how situations like this can get us to focus on how important our friendships and relationships are in fulfilling our lives. It can motivate us to take more opportunities to catch up with some people we haven't seen in a while and push us to make some new connections with people. Putting things off may cause regret later.

These types of situations make me ask myself many questions. What are we waiting for? Is there ever a perfect time when we have absolutely nothing going on? Why do we procrastinate on doing things that we could do sooner than later? How do we enjoy life and connections with others if we don't make the effort and devote the time to make things happen? How are we going to move beyond putting off those things we talk about doing?

There are times where we think we have all the time in the world to accomplish goals, forge relationships, and create a wonderful life. Unfortunately, we don't always see approaching difficulties or catastrophes. Life can become quite rough at times suddenly and without warning. Death and loss is a normal part of our lives and it can come up when we least expect it. Many times, we don't think that these situations are looming overhead until they happen to us. There are only a few absolutes in our existence, our death is absolutely one of them.

Considering our own mortality is something that almost everyone ponders during their lifetime, but I think it can be more important and impactful to consider what we are going to do while we are alive and how we want to spend our time. Focus on how to enjoy our lives and the people living around us while forming strong and exciting friendships. This can enrich our lives much more than fixating on the inevitability of death.

Although thoughts of mortality may concern us, many of us consider ourselves already stressed out and overwhelmed with other aspects of being alive. We can fixate on past situations, dream about how the future will be so much better than our current reality, or feel that our present-day issues keep us trapped. This stress can keep us from living a life we love living and stifle efforts to find those aspects of being alive that make us feel fulfilled and excited.

Our lives are in a constant state of trying to balance attention on the past, present, and future. Any of these can take too much of our concentration and energy. When this happens, we risk getting caught in one of them and losing focus on the other two that give us wisdom, motivation, and fulfillment. Finding balance in anything is easier said than done. Living in the moment, thinking about what his behind and in front of you, and being grateful for everything fantastic in your life can help to keep you motivated on what you are going to do to keep moving in a positive direction.

Remember, life truly is for the living. Be careful not to take it for granted because it can change in a heartbeat. It doesn't matter if you are putting off scheduling brunch, hanging out, or making out. Don't wait until you don't have the opportunity to do something that you wished you had done. Remember that each moment is important, meaningful, and precious.

Insights to impact your life

Our efforts to become healthier and happier people is a life-long journey that can be full of painful lessons, challenging catastrophes, and phenomenal successes. Through introspection, goal setting, and pushing ourselves to expand beyond our current actions and abilities, we create more opportunities to take control of our lives to feel more fulfilled, confident, and powerful. Here are some important beliefs that I feel can propel this process forward.

Clean out your closet.

Look at the attitudes, beliefs, and people that do not support your efforts to improve your life. Some things that we hold onto are unnecessary or counter-productive to our success. You can keep these types of items in the back of your closet forever, but consider throwing them away if they are ugly, don't fit, or you are tired of looking at them. Create space for some great new acquisitions.

Evolution is not always pretty, quick, or easy.

Transformations in our lives can take a long time and tons of energy, focus, and planning. It's important to not get demotivated because things take longer than we hope for or expect. This process takes as long as it takes, but there are things you can do to prompt these changes to happen quicker.

Doing things the same way doesn't necessarily mean that it is the right way.

Sometimes we just get stuck in a rut and can benefit from changing up our processes. If the same activities aren't getting you what you want, disrupt the status quo and see what happens when you do it differently. If it doesn't work, stop doing it.

Healthy relationships exist in many forms.

It doesn't matter if you are looking for new friends or

someone interested in a white picket fence lifestyle. Amazing people are all around us. It is important to be open to inviting the fantastic ones into our lives. Work on not being so rigid about what we think we need from people. Some may be awesome for hanging out while others can push us to try new things. Having a diverse group of people in our lives for a variety of types of relationships helps to keep things interesting.

The majority of limits placed on us are put there by us.

Be careful about getting stuck in thinking that you live in an oppressive environment where you can't change what is going on around you. Take the time to evaluate what you want to change and how best to achieve your goals. Many times we may feel powerless. Those feelings are often caused by multiple failures in our attempts to gain something. Don't let the fear of disappointment stop you from trying to be successful. These experiences can make us feel trapped, unhappy, and powerless.

If you want parts of your life to be different, make a plan and change.

As with almost all tasks, it is important to take the time and effort to analyze a situation, develop a series of activities designed to address the problem, get off the couch to try them out, and then evaluate how effective you were at achieving your goal. If you didn't win the coveted trophy, then modify what you did or try a different way to try to get what you want.

Don't get stuck in the past.

Learning from failures, challenges, and successes is extremely important so we are better equipped to kick ass in the future. It doesn't matter if you were a high school football star or a total dork, getting trapped anywhere in the past can stop us from being powerful in the future. Of course, past feelings of confidence and enthusiasm should be referenced as much as possible. Those positive beliefs are fantastic to get stuck in our minds, especially when things get difficult for us.

Evaluate what you are doing and why you are doing it.

If you are wasting energy on tasks, people, or situations that don't serve to improve your life or make you a better person, determine if this is really worth your time and efforts. There is nothing wrong about changing your tactics or your surrounding support network.

You have the ability to create the types of relationships you want.

After you have taken the time to figure out what kinds of people you want in your life, stick to your desires to have them take an active role with you. It can come in the form of a best friend, great sexual partner, travel buddy, or a brain-storming teammate. There is nothing wrong with putting in the time and effort to develop bonds with those people who improve your life.

Know yourself.

This really should be the primary goal for of our existence while we are living on this planet. It is the simplest idea that takes a lifetime to achieve. This knowledge of ourselves changes over time as we experience new and creative things. Sometimes slowing down to allow time to ponder possibilities or become unapologetically honest with ourselves is difficult for us. Achieving this type of personal enlightenment provides us additional motivation to go after our goals and dreams. It is important to know what we are fighting for.

ABOUT THE AUTHOR

Brent Heinze obtained a master's degree in clinical counseling and is a licensed professional counselor. His private counseling practice focuses on a variety of issues affecting gay men's quality of life. He is also a therapist and program director for an innovative behavioral health nonprofit in Denver that provides holistic wellness services. He created a nonprofit called Perspective Shift that focuses on supporting gay men's efforts in creating strong interpersonal relationships and making life changes. He strives to create an understanding of a world that can be confusing to many through professional insights as well as by discussing personal experiences and challenges.

In addition to his counseling efforts, he is an avid musician and creates music with his band Probe 7 and well as being a long-time member of Christus & the Cosmonaughts. He also runs a nonprofit called Lokusdor Productions that creates nontraditional fundraising events including an annual fetish ball that benefits organizations providing services and advocacy for LGBTQ and sex-positive communities. He currently lives in Denver with his husband Todd.

www.ingramcontent.com/pod-product-compliance
Lightning Source LLC
Chambersburg PA
CBHW062134280526
45788CB00001B/169